THE MAKING OF A
BUSINESS LEADER

My Path to Leadership in the
Information Technology Industry

RON NASH

ISBN 978-1-0980-7450-0 (paperback)
ISBN 978-1-0980-7451-7 (digital)

Christian Faith Publishing, Inc.
832 Park Avenue
Meadville, PA 16335
www.christianfaithpublishing.com

Printed in the United States of America

To Susan, who inspires me each and every day

CONTENTS

PREFACE

B ooks on business leadership fill the shelves of bookstores. Many people read multiple books and still cannot grow into good leaders. Leadership is driven by ego for many of these people, and ego is never a successful driver of a career.

To be a good leader, you have to make the commitment, you have to grow and improve yourself, you have to learn the skills of leadership, you have to drive yourself to produce, and you have to be a great servant leader who has a passion for helping others. These five topics are the basics of leadership, and what I focus on in this book.

In the poem *Ulysses*, Alfred Lord Tennyson says, "I am a part of all that I have met." That is certainly true for me and also true for us all. We learn from others and the people around us make us different—hopefully, better. All that I know of leadership has been learned from others. Without them, I would not have been able to progress.

In this book, I hope to allow you to learn through the experiences of my business career and through the great people with whom I have worked. They deserve the credit for my leadership skills. I am only the reporter of the important lessons which they have taught me. As an example of my continuing learning, I need to thank my colleague and good friend, Andy Maluish, for encouraging me to put these thoughts on paper by writing his book, *Working for Perot*.

I hope this book helps you in your quest to become a great leader. The world needs you as a great leader.

1

You Must Make the Commitment to Be a Leader

Accept the challenge

It comes to people at different times. Some people are thrust into leadership on an emergency basis and must sink or swim; some grow into it as their career develops; others make a decision to be a leader and work assiduously on it for years. For me, it was a teacher who took the time to make an observation that started me on the path for being a leader.

I was in the second or third grade at Conley Hills Elementary School in East Point, Georgia. I cannot pinpoint it or the name of the teacher because when my mother moved in her later years, the Report Cards of her four children were lost. In those early school years, we only knew printing, not cursive writing, so I could read my grades from my Report Card, but not the comments of the teacher. I asked my mother to read them to me. One comment was, "He shows leadership qualities." After she read that, I asked her, "What is leadership?" That abstract concept is not one that a young child can easily understand. She started explaining, and in my childhood way, I kept asking either why or what does that mean. She was having difficulty getting the concept of leadership across, so she said, "It means you could be like George Washington!"

That statement from my teacher via my mother hit me like a lightning bolt. I could be like George Washington, whom everyone admired and was a great person. I could be responsible for creating great things like he did—leading our army, helping found our country, being elected as our first president. Wow! That was exciting, but it was also scary. God had given me abundant talents that should be used to do great things. I needed to be different, and I needed to develop those talents.

That was my leadership challenge. That is the moment when I gained the confidence to be a leader and when I accepted the challenge of being the absolute best leader that I could be. At such a young age, being given the challenge to accept leadership positions is a great gift. It means you look at leaders to learn what they do. It means you readily accept leadership positions when they are available. It means that you start leading and learning at a young age when very few people have even thought of such opportunities or of developing themselves that way.

I wish that I could go back and thank that teacher. She gave me something that has defined my life and career. I thanked my mother for telling me that I could be like George Washington years ago. When I told that story, she had no memory of the conversation or even saying that. I showed her the report card, so she knew it was true and not a figment of my imagination, but it was just a passing comment to her. Just another way to teach a child. But it changed the trajectory of my life.

As I have gone back to the pivotal times in my life to thank people who ignited my passion and taught me important lessons, I have observed the exact same relative views of key events. They were life-changing to me, but they were just talking to my mentors. Almost none of my mentors remember giving me those valuable nuggets of wisdom that changed my life. They were just doing what good leaders do, passing along some advice to help someone.

In this book, I used those nuggets to highlight important lessons of leadership. Following that advice is how I earned my way to leading thousands of people, at times. In recounting how I got the advice and what I did with it, I hope to tell a story that will ignite your passion for leadership. The best way that I can honor those who helped me is to pass along their wisdom to you. Let's hope it works for you like it did for me—even better if possible.

I will admit that most of the leadership lessons cited in this book occurred early in my career. I did learn a lot then, but I am still learning today. It is more difficult to write of issues, problems and solutions, and to cite businesses and people that are still in the game today. Going back early in my career is safer. Most of those organizations and people have changed by now, so my talking in print about them will not be disruptive. Additionally, my target audience is people in the early stage of their careers. That is where I can make the most impact by changing the trajectory of a career in the early stages if people learn valuable lessons on leadership at that point. Those reasons are why the focus of this book is on lessons learned early in my career.

Just note that I am still learning and so should you. Never stop learning to be a better leader. You can never reach perfection, but you can strive to be as close to that as possible. The process is, sometimes painful, but mostly fun. And it is always rewarding to help others. Get after it ASAP and enjoy the journey. But do not expect success unless you make a lifelong commitment to leadership and to improvement.

2

You Can Improve Yourself

You can learn leadership; that is the important point. Sure, there are some traits that you have by birth or from the way you were raised, and those can help you be a powerful leader. For example, George Washington was tall and, typically, the tallest man in the room, so his height helped. But Napoleon was short, and he was a powerful leader.

You should understand the leadership advantages you were given by birth or having great parents like I did, but you should not rely only on them. Leadership can be learned over the course of your career and life. Unless you have a passion to be a great leader, it is not likely going to happen. You have to see yourself in that role, and you have to be comfortable in that role as you get leadership positions. But you also have to make a commitment to learn the lessons of leadership. In this chapter, we talk about some lessons of being a good leader, we describe what the lesson is, and we typically give some examples of how I learned those lessons.

So make the commitment to becoming a better leader and begin your study with this book. Learn these lessons and practice them. They do not become good habits until you do them over and over again. It is like learning a sport; first, you get the coaching, and then, you practice over and over again to develop the muscle memory of performing that sport. Only after it is in muscle memory do you become great. So start practice these lessons every day to get them to be habits that you just do without specifically thinking of them. Focus on them one at a time to get them ingrained as a part of you that is a habit. Then, you only have to focus on the issue at hand rather than thinking about how to be a good leader. That is how you become more powerful.

Have a little fun along the way

My grandmother, Mary Lorene Willkie Nash, was great about having fun each and every day. You might question this as an appropriate leadership lesson, but it is important.

My grandmother was usually happy and fun; her friends said she was a "card" which was a compliment for her spiritedness. It was also said that she was a "handful," meaning, she could be difficult as well. But as the first grandchild, she was always positive and helpful to me. In those more formal days, my mom called her mother-in-law "Mrs. Nash" rather than by her first name. As a baby, it was difficult for me to say "Mrs.," but I could say "Nash," so that is what I called my grandmother. It was not a sentimental name like most grandmothers have, but "Nash" reveled in her unique name and kept it throughout her life.

She always created a game out of any task. A simple task like gathering and sorting the clothes for the wash became a race as we each ran around the house to see who could pick up the most clothes the soonest and build the highest stack of whites or non-white dirty clothes.

The ability to have fun while you are working can be an incredible gift to a team. A leader cannot make every business task fun, but they can make some tasks fun, and they can laugh at themselves and others as they work together to create great results. All of us know the difference in how we feel when we go home at night after being productive, accomplishing some good results and having a bit of fun at work, versus when the day was just a grind. The grind absolutely wears on you; it saps your enthusiasm, your confidence, and your momentum. If you are tough, you can push through a grind for a while, but it is very difficult to sustain a good pace and develop a career when most days at the office are a grind. That atmosphere kills great teams.

So your first lesson is to lighten up and have some fun along the journey of your career. It will be sustaining for you and reenergizing for your team.

Look like a leader

After hearing of my grandmother, let's talk about what happened in the next generation. My grandfather had an eighth-grade education; my grandmother had a fifth-grade education. But they were both lifelong readers and were known as smart people. Reading is an essential, good lifelong habit in order to be a success.

My parents, Harold and Mary Anne Nash, were both exceptionally driven people. They came from similar lower-middle-class backgrounds and wanted to improve themselves and the lives of their children. Both of them recognized the very valuable role that education can play on the economic circumstances of a family. Each of my parents was the first in their family to graduate from high school. They graduated in the 1940s, as World War II was ending. They were also both leaders in their high schools; Dad played basketball (at a height of five feet seven and a half inches) and was elected as "Cutest Boy" in his senior class while Mom was captain of the varsity cheerleaders. You might wonder how I resulted from such visually appealing stock, but that is another story. Both were smart and made great grades in school. Mom even skipped a grade. She was so smart in the first grade that they promoted her directly to the third grade. Dad's crowning achievement in elementary school was the year that he made straight *A*s for grades—an *A* in every academic subject— while getting a failing grade for effort.

After high school, Dad enlisted in the US Army in order to qualify for the G.I. Bill to attend college. He volunteered for the paratroopers because their pay was twenty dollars per month higher. He got accepted only because he had a friend standing behind him in line lightly put his foot on the scale when they were weighing my dad. He was too light to join, but that was not how his weight was recorded. He had never even flown on an airplane until his first ride for his first jump. So he had to jump out of the first airplane on which he flew—pretty scary!

As he was finishing his military duties, Dad and Mom laid out a plan for him to get a college education with his goal being earning an electrical engineering degree from Georgia Tech. Since my grandparents could provide no financial help, it had to be self-financed. Their plan was to use the G.I. Bill for tuition, Mom would work during the day, and they both would work paper routes delivering the morning paper, *The Atlanta Constitution*, and the evening paper, *The Atlanta Journal*. Mom went to a predecessor college of Georgia State University for one year to take a secretarial course and obtain that certificate while Dad was completing his military duties. She began working afterward, and Dad was admitted to Georgia Tech. The first interruption in that plan came in the spring of Dad's freshman year when I was born. Obviously, this was something that required a revision to their plan. They decided—with my grandparents' participation—to let my grandmother keep me during the day while Dad went to school, and Mom worked. That worked in that they could keep their paper routes and Mom's job while I was being taken care of by my grandmother, Nash.

My mother told me that she collected for the newspaper weekly, on Tuesday evenings. People paid in cash and paid by the week at that time. She went house to house to collect. One Tuesday, Dad had a conflict with a class that he had to attend, so he could not keep me that evening. Mom took me on her arm and went collecting. She noticed that having a baby in her arms significantly improved the collection rate. People were not as eager to say they needed to wait another week to pay when she showed up with a baby. She began to take me from time to time on her collections route. I count this as my first business experience. I was only a prop, but I increased the Accounts Receivable collection rate!

Things went according to plan until Dad's senior year at Georgia Tech when my brother, Mike, was born that spring. Nash could not keep me and a newborn, so Mom needed to quit her job to stay at home with the two boys. That meant there was no money for Dad to finish his electrical engineering degree. He decided to drop out of college to get a job immediately and hoped to return someday to complete his degree and get a professional job. He went to the dean of students office to fill out the forms to withdraw from school. The dean of students at Georgia Tech then and for a long time afterward was George Griffin. He was one of those legendary personalities who stay at a college for their entire career and immeasurably help so many students.

Dad filled out the withdrawal form and went into the dean's office to get him to sign it. He told the dean why he was withdrawing from school. Dean Griffin asked him how much money he needed to stay in school, and Dad said "one thousand dollars," which was an impossibly large sum for Dad. The dean, then, refused to sign the withdrawal form. He said he could sign it the next day, but not that day. Dad got angry as he was due to start his new job the next day. Dean Griffin refused to budge and said, "Just come back to see me tomorrow."

That afternoon, Dean Griffin called several members of the Atlanta Rotary Club and raised a one-thousand-dollar loan fund. When Dad returned, Dean Griffin gave him a check for that amount and said no money would be due to be paid until he graduated from Georgia Tech and got a job. Dad was stunned. He could now finish college. Dean Griffin's generosity was incredible. It was the kind of act that he had done over and over again. He changed the trajectory of my parents' and my lives.

Dad graduated from Georgia Tech, repaid the loan, and later in life, joined the Rotary Club and served as its president. He did a massive amount of volunteer work and was always open to help someone in need.

As you can see, my parents were driven people. They advanced so far beyond where they had been raised. And they resolved that their children would advance even farther.

Like most father's, mine was regularly on me as a youngster to "stand up straight, look people in the eye when you are talking to them, shake hands firmly." That is not earthshaking advice. Most people are told precisely those things by their parents. But how many of us follow such advice?

When you are a leader, you are "always on." You communicate in a lot of ways—verbal and written. You understand those ways, but you also communicate messages when you are walking around the office. By the way, it is imperative that you do walk around so that you can see what is going on inside of your organization.

When you are walking around, everyone is watching you. Are you standing up proud and looking confident, or are you slumped over, looking down, and walking like you are under intense pressure?

I've spent a good part of my career in start-up organizations. Your feelings get whipsawed regularly when events happen. For example, when you get a call from a big prospect that they intend to purchase your product, you are on top of the world. You are feeling that your company is going to be a great success as are you. You can see yourself on the cover of *Fortune* magazine. Then, five minutes later, one of your big customers calls to say your software is not working, and they are thinking of stopping to use it. Now, you find yourself crouched in the corner of your office in the fetal position and shaking—five minutes after you were a big success.

The point is that you have high highs and low lows when you are building a business. You have to be able to moderate these feelings for your organization so that they can accomplish their work. You cannot let your emotional lows or your emotional highs distract the entire company from focusing on the tasks that they have to do each day to make the company a success. As the leader, you have to absorb the shocks and appear to be unfazed, and still focused on success when your team sees you.

Remember the famous lines from Rudyard Kipling's poem, *If:* "If you can meet with triumph and disaster, and treat those two impostors just the same." That is your goal as a leader. The leader stabilizes the organization so that it can function. Take a deep breath when you walk out of your office and put your game face on; it is important.

Ron with his parents

Act like a leader

Early in my career, I worked at EDS, Ross Perot's first great company. It was an information technology services company that pioneered the concept of outsourcing a function or a department for another company. They specialized in developing significant expertise and computer systems in areas so that they could convince companies that EDS could perform that function better and cheaper than the company could themselves. One of their sayings to a CEO was that the CEO should focus on the core functions of his business, and let EDS take the noncore functions and make them as efficient as possible.

In the early days of computers and business computing in the 1960's and 70's, there was a dearth of people who knew how to program or operate computers. One of Ross Perot's breakthroughs was that he had extensive internal training programs; one was called the systems engineer development program (SED), to graduate people who could write software. They were the early equivalent of the computer science programs taught in universities today. When you joined EDS, you first worked on an account which was a customer location where EDS was operating their computer systems. You got to see the good and the not so good business results that were possible, depending on how well the computer systems fit the business tasks. So before you ever learned about computing, you learned how it could help or hurt a business. This was an important insight to get into the heads of people we now call developers. They first had to learn the business functions.

After you worked in the business of a customer for a year or so, you were transferred to Dallas, Texas, where phase II of the SED program was given—the technical training. You spent a number of months in Dallas, learning computer languages and architecture design technique.

This enforced learning of both technical and business issues early in my career was invaluable for me as an individual performer and a leader. I also met one of the people who helped me the most at EDS. Glen Self, my mentor from EDS, said that the one thing that limits people in their career growth is the ability to handle uncertainty and still get their job done well. As a first-level employee, your world is very structured, and you can control a lot of the outcomes. Uncertainty is low. As you get promoted, you have to work through others which is both more difficult and more uncertain. As a CEO, I had massive factors in play that were uncertain. These uncontrollable factors could make me a success or a failure. But if I could not put aside that uncertainty and do my job each day, I was bound to fail. Glen's point is that when you get to a position where the uncertainty grips you and causes you distress, you are above your level of competency.

I once got to lead a company that was a turnaround opportunity. It had started as 1-800-Flowers and financially failed. We sold the flower business to Jim McCann who made that business a success, and we turned the original company around to be a call-center company, using the huge capacity that they had built (actually hugely overbuilt) for the flower business. Mort Meyerson was one of my investors there, and he was instrumental in getting me into Advanced Telemarketing to help grow that business. It was a scary time right after the financial failure, but with a lot of hard work by a great team, we got the call-center business growing well and doing well. It was the second largest call-center company in the United States at one point in time. Mort stayed in touch remotely, but he had not been out to our facility since the original financial crash. I wanted him to meet the team we had built and see all of the great improvements they had accomplished.

We hosted Mort on a visit, and my team was primed for impressing this legendary businessman as he spent time with us. The team presented to him superbly, and he was impressed. I could tell since I knew him, but my team was anxious to hear what he thought. When he was in our lobby, saying goodbye to everyone, he had still not given any feedback. He turned toward the door to walk out and, then, looked back at the leaders and me to say, "The stench of death has left this place." He, then, walked out.

My leaders were crushed. They did not know what to make of that, but I did. This was Mort 1.0 when he was tough and before his transformation. I had to reassure the leaders that this was a compliment and that they should be proud. Mort was positive on them. I think they mostly believed me, but not entirely. But we continued to grow the company, and we prospered.

All of these stories harken back to the lesson my father taught me, "Stand up straight, look people in the eye when you are talking to them, shake hands firmly." You have to do the work, but as a leader, you also have to play the part—every minute of the workday when you are at the office.

Be Texas direct

A leadership skill that Susan Nash, my wife, has is speaking directly to the important issues. She calls it being "Texas direct." She says that in Texas, people speak openly and directly to the issue, and that is why she is so fearless in addressing the real issue.

Some people call this "talking about the elephant in the room." Many people dance around the real issue because they do not want to confront people. They ignore the elephant in the room and talk about something else first. If you are going to be a good leader, you need to bring the important issue to the forefront quickly and directly so that everyone can deal with it.

Bringing up ticklish issues is not a negative; it is a positive. It makes everyone more effective. Just don't be afraid to bring up tough issues. Everyone generally knows that is the issue; they are just reticent to address it. Be polite and be respectful but be Texas direct; focus your team on spending its time working the most important issues and doing it as soon as possible. You can learn this skill, and it will carry you though a lot of tough situations. Start doing it today and make it a habit.

Learn how much you can push yourself

Leadership capability is determined by a host of factors such as knowledge, experience, emotional maturity, and intellect, but it is also determined by stamina—both mental stamina and physical stamina. Leading is a marathon, not a sprint, and stamina is very important.

We all know stories of executives who have failed because they had medical issues such as heart attacks. We know fewer stories of executives who have failed because of mental stress by having nervous breakdowns or turning to alcohol or drugs. There are multiple ways to fail under the increasing pressures which you will find yourself under as you progress to larger and more important leadership roles during your career.

A CEO with thousands of employees in a company does not get to do much direct work; they get to inspire, direct, organize, evaluate, etc., but they do not have their hands directly on almost anything that gets done or does not get done. They can live with this uncertainty as others are responsible for their success or failure. Taking an extreme example, think of a college basketball coach who is under intense pressure to win games, but the people who determine his success by doing work are teenagers. That coach carries a lot of uncertainty by having to depend on teenagers for his success, and he operates every day, carrying that uncertainty. That is a requirement for success.

There are various ways to toughen yourself up for the pressure that will come with career advancement. Some people have difficult childhoods and learn to be tough there. Some have intellectual challenges in growing up and learn to buckle down, work hard, and conquer challenges. Some have broken relationships or marriages which toughen them up. None of us, however, want to volunteer for difficult lives just to build our toughness.

So how do you build toughness? For me, a couple of things come to mind—team sports and military service.

Playing team sports as you are growing up is a great way to learn leadership qualities and to learn to work under pressure. You want to be the star yourself, but you also want to have the team win. You have to learn to balance these desires. None of us is always the star. All of us have a moment to shine on a team. When you play on a sports team, you are learning leadership lessons.

You also learn to work under pressure on a sports team. There are times when the entire team depends on you and how you perform—that is pressure, particularly for a child. I have heard that one of the single most difficult things to do in sports is to hit a baseball. Baseball is a team sport, but when you are batting, it starts as a one-on-one competition between the pitcher and the batter (or the bowler and the batsman if you want to use a cricket analogy). The pitcher is throwing the ball as hard as possible and with as much deception as possible. The time to size up the direction, pace, curve, and placement of a pitch is less than a second, and you have to already have the bat moving and in place to get a hit. It is a challenge. It is pressure. It is also a valuable leadership and development lesson to do this.

I played baseball for years as I grew up and was pretty good at it. I remember times when the team won and when I was a big part of it. I remember getting the winning hit or making the last out to win. You remember the good times, but you also remember the failures. You learn when you fail. I won some games for my team, but I remember one when I lost. My team was the Bears in Little League. We were behind by one run, and it was the bottom of the sixth inning, the last inning in a Little League game. There were two outs, but we had loaded the bases. I was batting third in the order which is the position where you place a hitter with good power and a good batting average. Batting with the bases loaded meant that all I had to do was get a solid hit, and we would likely win the game. I walked up to the plate confident. I had several hits that evening already, and I was confident that I could get another one and win the game for my team. The pitcher did not look confident; he knew I would be tough to get out. First pitch was a ball. The pitcher was worried about me and taking no chances. My confidence grew. The second pitch was good, and I swung—a miss for strike one. Next was another ball, so the count was 2 and 1. Next pitch was down the middle; I swung and missed again. I was stunned. I did not even foul the pitch. How could that happen? What did I do wrong? Now, 2 and 2. The next pitch was in the dirt so a 3 and 2 count. I was ready. I knew I could do it. The next pitch was down the middle and low. It was in my zone, and I could hit it. I swung—and missed. I was out. We lost the game.

It has been multiple decades since that game, but I can stand here today and see my bat going over that ball. I don't know how I could have missed on all of those three swings. It makes no sense to me. I can feel the shame and frustration right now that I felt on that day in Little League when I struck out. You remember the pain of the failures for a long time.

You learn the most from those failures. I was overconfident. I was on the edge of cocky. I was thinking too much of "the thrill of victory" rather than being intensely focused on doing my job. That is a life lesson. I learned at an early age that just because you are "expected" to win, you do not always win. That is a great business lesson. Each competition is independent, and you have to focus intensely to perform well over and over again. Each day is a new contest that you have to work hard to win. You can learn these important leadership lessons from team sports.

One of the great things that has happened in my lifetime is that women now have a chance to play team sports. Most opportunities to play team sports were for boys only when I was young, but the movement to open opportunities for women made a huge impact. Now, both boys and girls have an opportunity to learn to perform under pressure and to play as a team as a young age. That is a great thing, and one that will create more great leaders in the future—both male and female.

Another experience that absolutely toughened me up was military service. I served in the US Army, and my branch was the infantry. That is the group that is on the ground on the front lines in battle. I learned so much about leadership in the infantry; leading people when their lives and your life are on the line is a different type of pressure.

You start your military training in what is generally called basic training. This is the first step in turning men and women from civilians into soldiers, sailors, or airmen. It is a shock to your system and to your sense of yourself. The first shock comes right after you take the oath of office for the military when they remind you that you are no longer covered by the US Constitution and the Bill of Rights. Now, the Uniform Code of Military Justice rules over you, and things are different than in the civilian world. For example, when your superior officer gives you an order to "charge that hill" in battle, you don't have a chance to have a discussion with them about the danger of doing so. You just need to do it. If you don't, and if you turn around to run, the superior can force you to charge up the hill at the point of a gun. And they are not kidding around; they can legally use it on you. No trial by a jury of your peers. That adds a lot of pressure to your life every day. This is a serious business.

Basic training was mentally challenging to me as it was to others in that you have to get used to being in this new universe. The physical part was not as challenging to me because I was in shape coming out of college. In basic, there is a cross section of our country's people in your unit—tall/short, lean/fat, in shape/out of shape. So when you are running, the weaker of the people slow down the pace. For someone in shape, that makes the physical part doable. I could run easily, but I did have to build up my upper body strength significantly. Doing one hundred push-ups is pretty easy after you work up to it. Doing fifty chin-ups is a lot tougher, at least it was for me.

Once you complete basic training, you move to a school for your specialty. Mine was infantry. On the first morning of my infantry training, I fell out in formation before breakfast and started looking around at the other guys in training with me. There was not an ounce of fat on any of them. The slang term would be that they were a bunch of "lean mothers." This was going to be a physical challenge. That first morning, we ran over three miles with our rifles to the rifle range, before breakfast. Then, we ran back to breakfast. So six and a half miles running before we had breakfast. That was the start.

In infantry training, there is a huge physical component of getting you physically ready for hand-to-hand combat. There is also a significant mental component of getting you ready to perform under pressure in combat. They subject you to having to perform with the sounds, smells, and shocks of combat by making you physically crawl, walk, and run through fields where live bullets and explosions are going off. After the regular infantry training, we went to jungle training where they induce mental and physical stress by running you in the field without proper food. We were getting fed around six hundred calories a day for a couple of weeks which puts you under stress. That is where I learned to sleep standing up. When you are in a swamp for a couple of weeks, you cannot lay down to sleep; you would drown. So you lean against a tree and sleep. You can do it. Your body can cope. The jungle training days and nights were interrupted by "aggressors" attacking our position. So you did not have enough to eat or enough sleep, and you still had to perform. It is amazing what your body and mind can do when you push them. I went far beyond what I ever thought I could do in infantry training. It lets you see how strong your body and mind really are.

That infantry service made me a different person. I have a calmness under pressure and stress that I did not have before. I can focus and perform under great physical and mental stress. That is a great leadership quality.

Now, serving in the infantry is not everyone's cup of tea. I know that. You can learn to perform under stress other ways, and that is great. I learned stamina in getting my business degree from the University of Texas at Dallas when I worked a full day then went to class from 6:00 p.m. to 9:30 p.m. to learn about business. That was an effective but tough way to learn. The lesson is to put yourself in challenging situations in your career, over and over again. Volunteer for the difficult jobs. Try to do the impossible. Try to push yourself until you start to break. You are a lot stronger than you think you are. You can do much more than you think. You just have to push yourself to do it. Trust me, you can do it.

"Act like me"

Glen Self is one of the most talented and unusual people I have met in my business career. He is brilliant, driven, perceptive, aggressive, taunting, confident, and absolutely results-oriented. He has a PhD in operations research which is a higher-level mathematical modeling discipline that is very challenging to understand, much less to master. Ross Perot and Mort Meyerson wanted someone very smart to add to the team at EDS, and they recruited Glen as a vice president.

Glen led some business units like the Utilities Industry Center where I was part of the team in Connecticut. But his greatest value was that he was the ultimate cleanup leader. When something had gotten completely out of control and nobody could rescue it, Glen got the call. He had a very small team to perform this function that consisted of three other PhDs in operations research for whom Glen was their supervising professor in graduate school at Texas A&M. After we completed a project in Connecticut, Glen asked me to move to Dallas to join this team. I did not have a PhD, and I was only in my twenties, but he saw something in me that gave him confidence that I could contribute to this team.

Glen had a great sense of how much you could do, and he was the master of stretching you. I started to understand this as I was driving from Connecticut to Dallas through Atlanta, where my parents lived. I took off a few days to spend time with them and take my time driving to Dallas. It was Mardi Gras time, and I had never been to New Orleans, so I decided to drive through and stay one night there. It was a fun night as I went to some parades and had fun hanging out in the bars afterward. I got back to my hotel room at 2:30 a.m. There was a message waiting for me in my room (this was before cell phones existed). It was from Glen's administrative assistant saying that I had to go to an emergency meeting with Ross Perot the next morning in Dallas. They got me a ticket for a flight leaving at 6:00 a.m., then told me where Glen's car was parked at the airport. He had hidden a key, and they told me where it was. I was to drive his car to the EDS office, but they said to hurry because I had less than ten minutes to spare. Then, I could return to New Orleans that afternoon and drive my car to Dallas.

Wow. This was like being shot out of a cannon. I made the decision to shower at the hotel and, then, shaved with a blade in the small bathroom on the airplane. I found his car and the key and rushed into his office to pick him up so we could talk with Ross.

His admin handed me a pad of paper and a pen. She said, "You have three minutes to be in Mr. Perot's office. Glen left instructions to not tell him anything and to not commit to anything, but make sure you make him happy."

I asked where Glen was; she said he was out of town and had not planned to attend the meeting with me. Now, I was really scared, but I had no time to panic.

I got through my first one-on-one meeting with Ross Perot and back to my hotel. But if life with Glen was going to be like this, I was in for one exciting ride—and it was.

Now, to the story of the most valuable piece of career development advice that I ever had. This also came from Glen Self.

Glen was smart, but he was also combative. He liked to win, but he also liked to see the others lose. His approach to troubleshooting was to quickly—very quickly—assess the situation and discover the systemic solution to the problem. He never took short-term gains; he wanted to solve the issue for the long term. Once he had the issues and the solution determined, he would typically get the leaders of the team that allowed the problem to be created and fester together; then, he would tell them how dumb they had been and what they needed to do for the solution. These sessions were brutal. But he was inevitably right.

Glen and I had been working on a troubled area of EDS, and we had come to our conclusions of what needed to be done. The two of us were scheduled to fly together to the location and to present our findings and recommendations to the assembled EDS leaders. We got our flights and said that we would meet at the office that morning before heading to the airport.

When I got to the office, Glen told me he was not going. I said I could help cancel the flights. "No," he said, "you can go and present to everyone."

I said, "Glen, this is not going to work. I know how you present, and you are a VP and can carry it off. That room will be full of senior leaders of the company including three VPs. I am a twenty-year-old kid and cannot do the presentation."

Glen challenged me, "You know the material. You know the solution. You came up with a lot of it. You know what I would say and can do it."

"No, I can't. I know the subject, but those senior leaders will never listen to me. I can't present it like you would."

"How would I present it?"

Glen had a great sense of humor, so I went into a caricature of one of his presentations as he sat there and laughed.

"You helpless little idiots. You messed this up, and I have to bail you out again. Why don't you listen to me when I first tell you what to do? I am the great and powerful wizard of Self and am here to save you once again. Here is what you need to do, et cetera."

Glen laughed and said, "Just do that."

"I am telling you it will not work. They will throw me out of the room."

"You know the subject. Just go present like I would." Then, he said the kicker, "Act like me!"

That was the advice. I had a certain comfort zone where I could act. Glen's comfort zone was far more developed and broader than mine. But he was telling me to detach myself from my emotional and confidence limitations and to act like him. Just act like an actor in a play. I still did not think it would work, but I was beginning to understand.

I asked, "What happens if they get so angry at me that I get fired?"

"If you can be forceful enough for them to fire you on the spot, come in the next day, and I will rehire you with a thirty percent raise."

Wow. This guy was serious. I was scared, but I had to try this.

I did act like Glen, but truthfully, I toned it down a bit. But I was ten times more aggressive than I had ever been in a business presentation in my life.

Guess what? It worked! After my presentation, they were all over me, thanking me for bailing them out and telling them how they could solve these issues. I got congratulations from all of them. Not a single one thought I was arrogant or overbearing. I was stunned.

I learned a big leadership lesson. I was holding myself back. My confidence was lacking. I could do far more than I thought I could, if I could just get my confidence up.

I have used Glen's "act like me" advice over and over throughout my career. Whenever I see a leader doing a great job in a particular situation, I remember the situation and how the leader acted. When I am in a similar situation, I detach from my normal style and use the style that I saw that leader use that was so effective in that particular situation.

We all learn from others, but this is learning at a different level. Just adopt the style of the leader and think of yourself as an actor in a play rather than as being yourself. It means you can develop an incredibly broad set of skills and styles. Sometimes, you need to be consultative; sometimes, you need to be directive; sometimes, you soar and inspire people for greatness; other times, you tell them the hard facts of reality.

Glen's "act like me" advice has made me so much broader and so much better of a leader. I have found that after you "act like me" several times, that style then becomes part of you. It is part of your tool kit and no longer feels like you are acting.

What a great leadership lesson. Just imitate a leader whose style fits the opportunity. Act like me.

IT Industry Insights
Services Businesses Require Intense Leaders

Service contracts, such as IT and business process outsourcing, are inherently unstable. The instability over time comes because once the service vendors solve the key problems that led to the outsourcing, the customers quickly forget that they were not producing when they were leading the operations. So they want to take the operations back in-house. In order to keep these contracts stable over a long time, the outsourced operations require skilled leadership that is hands-on, intensively committed to success, creative about crafting business solutions, and great at motivating large teams. All industries need good leaders, but service industries need the subset of leaders that are stylistically relentless and who are great people leaders.

The reason is that these contracts require the service business to perform better every day than the company that outsourced part of their business to the service company. That is a tall order. It can be achieved, but it will not unless the service business, its leaders, and all of its workers have a deep commitment to be better every day in every way.

Most of these service contracts are structured with a base fee and variable fees that move according to the amount of work done. To make the margin targets that service companies have for their business, the service company has to first satisfy the business needs of the customer that outsourced the work to them, then they need to maximize the work that is done, both increasing volumes of current transactions as well as finding additional projects that can be done to benefit the customer. To do this well, the service company needs several layers of leaders with the same positive, evangelical style of leadership that motivates teams to push for more production and to dig for new projects aggressively. These companies cannot be managed from above by making a few big decisions; their success is based on making numerous little decisions that each contribute a part to their overall success.

It is a cliché, but there is some truth to be learned from the saying that most of these service businesses are based on billing for manpower and that the way to success is to motivate your team members to work more than eight hours a day so that you can bill for those additional amounts while you pay your professional staff a fixed salary. That generates additional revenue at no incremental cost which creates your margin.

The business truth is that outsourcing part of a business is a leap of faith for a customer to do. Accepting the idea that an outside company can perform better than their own people is difficult. The burden then shifts to the service company, not just to perform on the contract, but to delight the customer regularly by doing extra work that adds significant business value for the customer. The extra ideas and projects that add value are what makes the service contract stable and enduring. Without these extras, service contracts blow up over time as the customer forgets the problems that the services company solved and decides that they could take the work back in house and do a better job.

I have seen services businesses work very well in the case of EDS, Perot Systems, and ATC. At these places, we had top leaders who had this intensity and creativity as their leadership style. We also had middle-level leaders with the same intensity and creativity. We also had team members with the same intensity and creativity. Our teams did what the contracts required and relentlessly worked to find other ways to add value to the customer. These extras proved to the customer that the decision to outsource was the right one and they also generated the margin to make these contracts valuable to our company.

In addition to experiencing the right way to make these contracts work, I have seen two cases that proved that the lack of this intense leadership destroys service contracts and companies over time. When Hewlett Packard acquired EDS to add to their services business, they managed EDS like it was a hardware manufacturing business. Of the two hundred top executives of EDS at the time of the acquisition, HP terminated or lost 90 percent of them in the first eighteen months. That is several layers of leaders removed. The specification to the search firm to replace these leaders was to recruit leaders at half the compensation of the EDS leaders. HP did this and they got regular business leaders, not the intensive/creative leaders like EDS had. Three years after the acquisition, HP's services business from EDS was not growing and not profitable. The combination of not optimizing their existing contracts, not signing enough new contracts, and losing too many of their current contracts led to this destruction of a healthy business. After several years, HP divested the EDS services business at a loss by combining it with CSC to form DXC. Leadership counts and having the right type of leadership for a business is very important.

A second incident showing this same pattern comes from Dell that acquired Perot Systems. They were also a hardware manufacturer like HP and they made very similar decisions about how to manage Perot Systems after it was acquired. These decisions, particularly removing several layers of leaders from Perot Systems, led to the same business result of not enough growth and not enough profitability. Several years later, Dell sold this services business at a loss to NTT Data.

One of the most telling anecdotes of a leader from a hardware company not understanding the services business came from a conversation between a senior Dell executive and a senior leader at Perot Systems. They were working the normal business process of planning the budget for the next year. The Dell executive said that for the next year's budget, they needed more revenue and less costs than the prior year. The Perot System's executive said, "You mean more revenue and more margin, right?" The Dell executive said, "No, more revenue and less total cost." This confrontation shows the difference in their experiences. The Dell executive was a good leader for a manufacturing business where you grow revenue each year and you push hard to decrease your overall manufacturing costs, thereby creating more margin in your products. The Perot

Systems executive was a good leader for a services business where you grow revenue each year, but when your delivery mechanism is people, you increase your total expenses. More margin is created by increasing prices and gaining leverage on your people's efforts, not by decreasing the total number of people. If you cut the number of people to save costs, you remove the chance to do the work that satisfies the customer and sustains the services contracts. This was a classical example of competent leaders coming from different backgrounds not communicating well and not making the right business decisions.

These are simple examples of the important point which is that you need the right type of leader for a business. For services businesses, you need leaders who have the intense evangelical type of leadership that highly motivates a large team to strive to delight the customer each and every day. Without this type of leadership, the services company will not succeed.

Don't let success breed arrogance

My first job after the military was with EDS which was a very successful company. Ross Perot had pioneered a whole new industry segment, information technology services, and had dominated it. He took EDS public on the New York Stock Exchange in the late 1960s, with the help of Ken Langone and his small investment banking firm, at a valuation higher than had ever been seen—and he sustained it! It was one of those companies that creates a new segment and dominates it for decades.

EDS in the early days recruited primarily from people who had been in the military; they were older, more mature, more settled, and more skilled in leadership than were typical college graduates. So you coupled a very successful company with very successful people, and you got a combustible mixture. With all of this success, it was very easy to believe that there was something special about you and that the rest of the world should just get used to dealing with you on your terms!

Obviously, this is not a sustainable business positioning. Years later, Mort Meyerson in his version 2.0 regularly cautioned the talented people at Perot Systems to not let success breed arrogance. Success is great, confidence is great, enthusiasm is great, but when it steps over the line to become arrogance, it is very, very dangerous. Remember the Aristotelian warning, "Every virtue carried to an extreme is a vice."

You may have the pleasure of working for a great company that is doing great, working with talented people. and having your career be on a rocket ship headed for the top. Enjoy it while it lasts, but you cannot and must not believe that you are that special or that you are the catalyst for this positive combustible mixture. There will be times when it works like this and times when it does not. Keep your perspective and humility when you are in the good times.

There was a very successful database company called Sybase. It was the hottest of the hottest for a number of years. It grew, IPOed, and kept on growing. The people of Sybase thought they were very special and that this would last forever.

They did not notice a small start-up company that also had a database software product that had one technological advantage over them; it was a relational database rather than hierarchical. The name of that little company was Oracle. The technology industry repeats this pattern over and over again. Companies get successful, and they miss seeing a new technology that, ultimately, can kill their company. Oracle was the most successful database company ever. When you are successful, keep your eyes open for competitors who are doing something differently. That might be a warning for you.

When I was at the call-center company, ATC, we had pioneered a number of technologies for our industry. We were the first to connect our telecommunications switch with our computer system so that we could put a screen on the desktop of a sales representative, at the same time that we put the call on their headset. This meant that we could see the phone number that the client had dialed and also could see the phone number from which they dialed, and we could use that information to put the appropriate information and script in front of our sales representative. We had other technology advantages, but this was one of the best and most productive. It meant we could put calls from multiple companies into one group of representatives and obtain the economies of smoothing out the demand from all of the companies and achieve the benefits of consolidation in our profitability. We had a talented IT group, and our technology created business value for us.

One day, the VP and chief information officer at ATC came into my office. He said that a salesman had been in earlier that day with his new software product and that our team had evaluated it versus our current technology. He said that our current technology was better than the software that the salesman had presented, so he did not see a fit in using them. He recommended that we pass on further evaluations of the new software. Without any questions or much thought, I said that I agreed and to turn off the effort of looking at the new software.

Two years later, I learned the name of the salesman who had visited our company—Tom Siebel. If you are an IT person, you will recognize that name as the founder of Siebel Systems, which pioneered the customer relationship management segment. Siebel was a very successful company that grew to be worth many billions of dollars. This meant that, at a point in time, my company had software that was better than Siebel's, but we saw the market as technology for our own call-center company. Tom saw another market for that technology that was far larger—helping every company to manage their customer relationships.

You can say that our success and arrogance led us at ATC to not really listen to what Tom Siebel was saying and to evaluate what he was doing. It meant that we missed a giant business opportunity because we were so focused on our own much smaller opportunity. Tom had a better business model for creating value.

Another story of inflated ego and arrogance that I like comes from a very successful Dallas businessman, Dick Bass. Dick regularly told this story on himself, so I feel comfortable in relaying it.

Dick was successful in business as an early investor in the Vail Ski Resort and the owner of Snowbird ski resort. He was one of those few people who had climbed the Seven Summits, the highest peaks on the seven continents:

- Africa—Mount Kilimanjaro
- Europe—Mount Elbrus
- North America—Mount Denali
- South America—Mount Aconcagua
- Asia—Mount Everest
- Antarctica—Vinson Massif
- Australia—Mount Kosciuszko

In fact, Dick was the first person to achieve this, which he did in 1985 after he successfully scaled Mount Everest. He had climbed the other six peaks by 1983. This is a very dangerous mountaineering achievement, and one of which you should be very proud of accomplishing.

Dick's story is that he was flying in first class on American Airlines from New York to return home to Dallas one afternoon. That is about a four-hour flight. He sat down and quickly started talking with the guy sitting next to him. Dick said the guy was very interested in what he had done and had a lot of questions about climbing and the effect on the body of altitude. Dick said that they had a very animated four-hour discussion.

It is an odd human trait, but I have noticed many times that you get in conversation with a person on a flight and have a great conversation, but you don't introduce yourself to each other, until right as you are about to leave the plane. Once you stand up in the aisle, you say something like, "I really enjoyed talking with you. By the way, my name is Ron Nash." Then, that person introduces themselves to you.

That happened to Dick Bass on this flight. As they were standing up to leave the plane in Dallas, he introduced himself and the person said, "I enjoyed hearing about your mountain climbing and talking with you. My name is Neil Armstrong."

Neil Armstrong was the first person to walk on the moon. Dick Bass had him captive for four hours and says, "I did not ask him a single question or give him a minute to talk. What an arrogant idiot I was!"

Don't let your confidence grow into arrogance. That is when you miss opportunities. Keep yourself on the ground and keep your eyes and ears open for learning. Then, you can continue to grow.

Mort 1.0 to Mort 2.0

Mort Meyerson is a leader and friend for whom I have worked at EDS, ATC, and Perot Systems. He is unusual in a number of ways, but one of the most profound is that he has had a career where he was radically different at different stages of his life. In his early life, he was smart, hard-charging, aggressive, pushy, combative, etc. Later in his life, he executed a transformation to become just as smart but contemplative, creative, supportive, caring, etc. He achieved great business results with both leadership styles, but with the later one, he built a far stronger team. I have known very few people who could transform themselves as well as their business and individual person-alities so dramatically, and to do this later in life is very impressive.

A couple of anecdotes from my times with Mort can illustrate the two well-defined but radically different styles. Early in my career at EDS, I was working in New York City where Ross Perot had pur-chased two investment banking firms—DuPont Glore Forgan and Walston & Co. In a recession, these banks had become insolvent, and the president at that time, Richard Nixon, called Ross Perot to purchase them. He was worried about such large investment banks failing and wanted them in stronger financial hands. This is eerily similar to the "too big to fail" recession at the end of the George W. Bush administration when similar concerns surfaced.

Mort was the account manager of the EDS-outsourced infor-mation technology contract for DuPont Glore Forgan, and when Ross bought it, he appointed Mort to be the CEO of the investment bank. Mort was in his thirties and was an IT professional, not an investment professional, but Ross trusted him to rebuild this company. Later, Ross decided to merge DuPont with Walston & Co., the second investment bank he had purchased. Trying to get synergies and economies of scale was the business reasoning behind the merger.

I was a very new EDS employee, and Mort sent me on a mission. In San Francisco, both investment banks had offices. The Walston office was downtown on Montgomery Street in the financial district in an old building. It was packed with people, crowded, old, needing restoration, and very profitable. The DuPont office was high up in the new Bank of America building, with lots of private offices and a magnificent view of the harbor, the Golden Gate Bridge and the Bay Bridge. It had luxurious furnishings, extra space, and was nowhere near profitability. My mission was to analyze the likely results if you consolidated the offices in one or the other location. Obviously, everyone would love to be in the nicer offices, and conversely, some brokers might resign if shoehorned into the cramped Walston office, so you needed to forecast that. You also needed to look at the leases, the costs, the effects on morale, etc. Mort wanted to know what he should do in selecting the location for the consolidated office.

I spent several days talking with people and doing the analysis very privately. I read documents and made assumptions and forecasts. In a surprise, once I forecasted the profit and loss for each location over several years, neither one came out ahead. If you consolidated down to the old Walston location, you lost production and were smaller, but you were profitable immediately. If you moved everyone to the luxury office of DuPont which was larger, it took you a bit of time for the profits to catch up. But on a five-year basis, the financial performance was essentially the same. That was an unusual conclusion, but that is what the data said.

I typed my report and consolidated it to one and a half pages for an executive summary. It told Mort that, financially, it made no difference. Therefore, he could make the decision on other factors like cultural—be a nice guy and move to the luxury location—or send a strong message about the importance of profitability by being frugal in the old office. I talked with Mort's administrative assistant, and she told me to meet him at the Mark Hopkins Hotel in San Francisco to give him my report after he finished a dinner meeting around 9:30 or 10:00 p.m. As an eager new employee, I posted myself early outside of the dining room and waited for Mort to emerge, so I could give him my report. He came out, I handed him the report, and he stood there to read it. He made a couple of sounds, "Humm, uh-huh, okay." Once he finished reading the report, he said, "That's what I thought." He, then, tossed my report on the ground, stepped on it, and walked off.

I was crushed. Did I do something wrong? Was my job in jeopardy? All these negative thoughts crossed my mind. I picked up my report with Mort's footprint on it, went back to my hotel, got in bed, and tried to go to sleep. At around 4:30 a.m., Pacific time, my phone rang. It was Mort's general counsel at DuPont in New York. He said, "Ron, Mort called me last night and said he had the most incredible experience. He has been listening to all of this posturing and political gamesmanship around the office selection decision. He said it has been very political and very painful. Then, last night, he said one of the new young employees of EDS gave him a report that cut through all of the games and gave him one of the most succinct business recommendations he had ever read. He said I had to get a copy of that report so I could read it, and we could take action on it immediately. He wanted the board to see this."

Wow. What a turnaround. From worrying about losing my job to being a superstar in just a few hours. That is how I felt. But the story here is how tough Mort was. He expected everyone to be excellent, and when they were, that was just doing their job. There was no need for flattery or compliments. Just do your job and do it very well. That was the original Mort style. I understood his focus on excellence and was okay with him setting a very high standard like that. It caused me to always strive for greatness, not just competency.

Years later, after EDS had been sold to General Motors, and Ross, Mort, and two other officers, Bill Gayden and Tom Walter, had been asked to leave; Mort looked back on the EDS experience and not positively. He was introspective and saw that his overwhelming commitment to work and lack of any balance in other parts of his life did not make him or his family happy. He wrote a very critical article for *Wired Magazine* called "Everything I Knew About Business

Was Wrong." In it, he asked, "Do you have to be miserable to create wealth?"

When Ross Perot ran for president, he asked Mort to come into Perot Systems as CEO to replace him. Mort did that but resolved to do things differently this time. Mort was less abrasive and much more friendly and supportive. He was fun to be around while we were working. He started writing about what he was doing and emailing these stories to the people who reported to him. They were part business communications, part travelogue, part food and wine reviews, etc. Others started doing the same thing. At EDS, nobody wanted to ever talk about anything other than business. To admit that you had other interests was looked at as a sign of weakness. Now, Mort was changing that culture at Perot Systems.

He did, however, make a mistake once. We hosted the executive team of a prospective customer at our headquarters in Dallas for a comprehensive presentation on how we could help them. The CEO was outspoken, arrogant, and opinionated during the presentation. At the end of the day, they left, and one of our teams sent around a copy of the slides that we presented to everyone attending, the Perot Systems team, plus the executives from the prospective customer. Mort saw that email and "replied all" to it, thinking it was only sent to the Perot Systems people. In his reply, Mort said, "Wasn't that guy an asshole?" Well, he was, but sending that note to him was a mistake. Obviously, we did not get that contract.

I learned from Mort 2.0 that if you show your team your personality and that you had broad interests, it was reinforcing for your leadership. The more they saw you as a person, the more they could relate to you and could put your business advice and requests in perspective. I have used this lesson ever since learning it from Mort. You are the leader, but you are also a person, and you need to relate to your team on multiple levels. Those robust relationships can help bond people for the long haul and make teams work together, hand and glove. It makes them perform better which is always the goal.

Changing a company in substantial ways like their business model is difficult; changing yourself in substantial ways is even more difficult. Mort Meyerson showed me that you can change yourself in fundamental ways to make yourself even more effective and successful. Always keep your eyes open for better ways to do things, and never underestimate the power of a human being to change. You can do it and you can become even more powerful.

Information Technology Icon: Mort Meyerson

Mort Meyerson was president of EDS and, later, CEO of Perot Systems, beginning when Ross Perot ran for president. Mort is a right-brained person in a left-brained business world. He learned to be tough and was one of Ross Perot's most aggressive leaders, but he was also one of the more creative people in those companies; many of the engineers called him weird rather than creative, but you know how little engineers appreciate unstructured ideas. I learned leadership lessons from Mort 1.0 in the EDS days and from Mort 2.0 in the Perot Systems days. Both were valuable for me in my career.

Mort is one of my favorite people, and it is always entertaining watching him disrupt discussions with different ideas—some good, some bad, but all worth considering. Mort 2.0 had a great sense of humor about himself. An example of this occurred at one of the leadership meetings at Perot Systems. Mort was on stage and talking about how we needed to align our teams better and to get them enthused about our future opportunities. He was grasping for words when he said, "We need to have one of those meetings, like at church when the music plays louder, and everyone gets excited. What do you call it?"

From the audience, someone said, "A come-to-Jesus meeting."

"Exactly," Mort said, "that's what we need."

From the audience, someone else said, "Mort, what do you know about come-to-Jesus meetings, since you are Jewish?"

Mort smiled and said, "I stood up at a come-to-Jesus meeting. I was one of the only Jewish football players on the Paschal

High School football team in Fort Worth. The coach took the entire team every Sunday night to the church service at the First Baptist Church. The part of the service that I enjoyed was at the end with the loud music when they asked people to stand up to commit their lives to Jesus. I was sitting in a pew, and my two friends on either side of me lifted me up when they made the call. So I do know what a come-to-Jesus meeting is."

Mort's smile and surprising personal story captivated the audience. It was a great touch of a great leader.

In the early years of EDS, the company was successful in signing a number of contracts with various states in the United States to automate the administration of Medicare and Medicaid plans. EDS was in process of developing a new software system to do this. They were near signing the state of California to a long-term contract to provide the services and were facing persistent questions from officials in California about how a small company like EDS could do a better job than the hundreds of people that the state currently had working on developing a system. This objection was getting into the way of winning the business.

Mort Meyerson was one of the leaders working on signing this contract, and in the discussions at EDS on how to best counter this objection, he came up with a new idea—what if EDS brought all of the current employees of the state of California over to become EDS employees upon signing the contract? This would give EDS far more people to develop the software and would assure the state that EDS would, then, have many employees who were very knowledgeable about the needs of the state of California.

This idea allowed EDS to sign the contract with the state. It also was a first instance of a new business method that we currently call outsourcing. Now, EDS did not name this outsourcing; they just used this method over and over again to grow their employees as they signed new contracts. They called it facilities management, a term which never moved to general usage, and they switched to calling it outsourcing years later, when that term came into general usage. But Mort lays claim to being the Father of Outsourcing after the contract with the state of California signed. That is a very impressive accomplishment to pioneer a new business method that leads to a huge new industry that grows for decades.

What is the big leadership principle that Mort used that you can learn? It is that when you are working to do something new, you have to be absolutely open to using new business methods to capture large opportunities. You cannot just do things the same way over and over again, even if that way worked for you previously. You need to be objective about the strengths and weaknesses of your current business methods and creative enough to craft entirely new methods to capture sizable new opportunities.

Many large companies fail to vary their business methods and become vulnerable to smaller, more agile competitors with new business models. A clear current example of this is the taxi companies who had a captive market with a business model but failed to see that a new business model, pioneered by Uber, could capture most of their market. Uber had a better business model, and one that no incumbent taxi company had adopted. Don't be blinded by your prior success; you may be missing out on opportunities if you are not brave enough and creative enough to change your business model as the business situation changes. That is a leadership principle that you need to learn and use over the course of your career.

Mort Meyerson 2.0
Photo courtesy of Chris Ronan

3

Learn the Skills of Leadership

As you advance in your career, you need to learn the specific lessons of leadership. You can learn these lessons from leadership books, you can learn from leaders around you, you can learn from people at other companies, you can learn from reading business history books; there are a lot of ways to learn. When I was early in my career, I learned from looking at the leaders above me in the business organization. I saw what they did well and did not do well.

Once I became a CEO for the first time, I had nobody in the organization to look up to on a daily basis to learn. I had a board that helped me, but I could not learn every day. Then, I found something very surprising; I could learn from people lower in my organization. That view of mine to look above could be reversed to look below, and I could learn a lot of leadership lessons. People in my organization did some magnificent things, far better than I could have done, and I learned a lot from them.

The key is to always be learning. Never stop. Never be satisfied. You can always learn. Focus on learning how to be a leader, and it will help you immensely. Learn how to be a great leader.

Act fast and fix the systemic problem first

One Saturday morning, I got a call from Glen Self. He said Ross Perot and he had another turnaround mission for me and to come

45

into the office on Monday morning with a bag packed. I asked about what the mission was, where it was—all of the normal questions. He only told me to pack work clothes for one week and that they would meet me at 8:30 a.m., Monday, in Ross's office to tell me what they wanted me to do. Then, I would fly out to the site.

On Monday, I learned that one of the state Medicare and Medicaid contracts was in deep trouble. EDS had a contract to process the claims for this state for its federally mandated but state-administered health-care programs. The situation was dire:

- EDS had operated the contract to process claims for nine months, and they were seven months backlogged in paying claims.
- The governor of the state had called Ross to tell him that the major hospitals in his state were near bankruptcy because they were providing medical services under these programs and were getting no reimbursement because EDS was not paying their claims.
- The governor said that if this situation did not improve quickly, like in a couple of weeks, and in large part, then, he would publicly denounce EDS as incompetent and sue to revoke the long-term contract that was in place.
- And if this was not enough bad news, this single contract was losing money at a rate that, if continued, would consume 50 percent of EDS's profit for that year. Reducing their earnings by half would result in their public stock price plummeting, losing billions of dollars for their stockholders.

My mission was to fly there, take charge quickly, and start making progress fast. Glen handed me a plane ticket to the state capitol city. The flight was leaving in ninety minutes.

Ross firmly added the following admonition, "I want you to make progress each and every day on improving the performance. I also want you to call me at 5:30 every afternoon to tell me what you did that day that made this account more profitable, not in the future, but that day. I don't want to hear plans or intentions of future profits. I want to hear how much more profitable we were that day due to your actions. Call Barbara every day at 5:30 p.m., and she will put you in to talk directly with me."

"Yes, sir!" What else could you say?

I headed to the airport. I started to think about the situation and how these contracts worked. EDS would receive claims from hospitals, doctors, or individuals. These were entered into their computer system where a determination was made of the validity for the claim. If it was valid and the billing fit the tables for that medical procedure, the claim went to be paid and a check was produced. If it was not valid (a simple example would be that the procedure was for an amputation of a leg, and it was the third one for that patient), then, the claim would be rejected with an explanation printed out for the submitting party. If the computer system could not determine the validity automatically, the claim was kicked out to a group of medical professionals for them to make the proper determination of the validity. Obviously, you wanted most claims to be administered in an automated fashion because that was fast and cheap. Once a human had to review the claim, the costs of running the program dramatically increased.

On the EDS revenue side, they were paid a fee for each claim that was paid or rejected. So they were also interested in claims going through the system fast and without that human intervention. In this case, the solution to the governor's issues and to EDS's internal profitability issues were the same. We need to be adjudicating more claims quickly.

I knew nothing about what caused these issues, but I knew what the systemic fix was—get claims processed quickly, accurately, and with as little human touch as possible.

I checked my flight schedule and figured that I would arrive at the account at 3:30 p.m., Dallas time. That gave me two hours to make something happen so that I could call Ross that day. Now, most people would think that they had time to do some analysis that first day, but I knew that this was a test by Ross and that he wanted me to call him that day. That was a big challenge, and I was primed to find something fast that I could implement and make it happen before I called Ross.

I came to the account and went to the office of the EDS account manager. He was not expecting me. Nobody had told him who I was or that I was coming. This would have been unheard of in most companies, but EDS in those days was freewheeling and did things like this. Ross and Glen were both action-oriented and always wanted to get results as soon as possible, whether they disrupted the company hierarchy or not.

I met the account manager and told him, "Ross and Glen sent me from Dallas to get things working in this account fast. I will be here and will be in charge until things are working smoothly; then, we can go back to the normal organization. Until then, you work for me as does everyone here. Let's get started."

He was taken aback, but he knew enough of the company's methods, and of Ross, to not discount that this was true. He said, "I hear what you are saying, but before I can start working for you, I need to verify that from my manager. I am sure you know that I have to do that."

This started a delay process that went on over an hour, as he could not contact his manager or the next level up. I told him that I could call Ross Perot and put him on the phone with us as a quick way to get authorization, but he did not want to do that.

We had killed a lot of time, so my objective of making a first-day impact was not looking good. I had to do something more dramatic to get this moving. I asked the account manager's administrative assistant if she had an organization chart for the account. She did, and she gave me a copy.

As the account manager was in his office on the phone, I looked at the organization chart and saw the solution! In three places, there was an unusual pattern, like the one below:

Account Organizational Chart

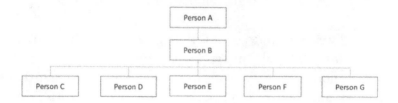

At three places in the organizational chart (there were about four hundred fifty people on the account at this time, plus others in training), the unusual pattern of Person A and Person B occurred. I looked at them and marked a circle around the boxes for Person A and Person B. By now, we had less than an hour until I had to call Ross with my results.

The account manager came out and said, "It is late in the day, and I am unlikely to get one of my managers on the phone today. What don't you go check into your hotel, and we can go to dinner tonight to talk about this. I expect to get one of the managers later tonight or tomorrow morning, so we can start working on this tomorrow."

"No, that is not going to work. But I have something which we can do today to get this account more profitable. Look at your organization chart. Look at these three odd arrangements of Person A and Person B. I don't know either of these two people but either Person A is so weak that he can only lead one subordinate, and he needs to be fired, or Person B is so weak that he needs someone to manage him full-time, and he needs to be fired. If you can tell me who is the problem person in each of these circles, we are going to fire the weak one today and let the other one lead the group."

Now, a complicating factor was that this account manager's name was in one of circles! He was a Person A type, and he had only one person reporting to him who managed everyone else in the account.

He replied, "I see your point, but we are not going to do that today. I don't even know who you are, and to fire people because some unknown person walked into my office is ridiculous."

"So we agree that the situation in all of the circles is intolerable and needs to be corrected."

"Yes, I can agree with you on that, and I was working to get it done."

"So all we are talking about is timing. You can verify who I am by calling Ross. Let's walk into your office and do that."

"I am not comfortable with firing someone until I can verify that this is working. I need to talk to my managers, not Ross Perot."

This is the kind of bureaucratic behavior that I knew infuriated Glen and Ross, as well as me. We needed to be more agile and more aggressive. So I decided that I needed to push him into action by telling him that unless he would tell me the weak person in each circle, I would choose one to fire. He did not take me seriously, so I started to walk out into the account office, asking people where one of the people was. He followed me and said, "You are about to fire the wrong person."

I said, "Okay, then, will you fire the right one?" He said yes, and we made our impact that afternoon.

He fired two people, and for the one person under him, he told him he would be transferred to another account within EDS that day. He said that person was very good, and he wanted to save him for the company.

I was okay with that. It was now 5:20 p.m., and I called Ross. "Ross, today, we moved three nonperformers off this account, and we will do more tomorrow."

Ross said, "That is great, Ron, and exactly what I wanted to hear. Glad that you are being a hard-charger and getting things done. I'll talk with you tomorrow."

Now, this sounds very aggressive, bullying, and belittling. I know that. But this was years ago, and EDS was a very successful company with a very combative culture. When I was in the infantry, we, sometimes, played volleyball. At the start, we would agree that we were going to play using regular volleyball rules or "jungle rules." Most of the time, we played using jungle rules, which means you can do a lot of rough things to win. For example, when a person on the other side of the net went up for a block, you could punch your fist through the net to hit their exposed chest, or you could dive under the net to take them out with a roll block. This was full contact volleyball. You could not grab the net to lower it, but a lot of other physical behavior was acceptable. In those days, EDS played by jungle rules, internally. It was rough, but it was very effective in letting the strongest leaders and strongest performers rise in the organization.

This culture—looked at through the lens of today—is, obviously, not a great way to lead a business or to treat people. I agree. But this was an emergency situation, and I needed to make a point that, to use a Texas phrase, "There was a new sheriff in town."

We had to quickly establish that we were going to move at a different pace and that doing business as usual was unacceptable. The leadership lesson is that you always want to treat people respectfully and do things with the long term in mind. However, in crisis situations, you have to get momentum going toward solving problems quickly. You have to do whatever it takes to establish that things will be different, and things will be better—and soon.

Let's continue with this example and talk about the systemic solution that I thought about on the flight into the account because it is important that you learn this. When I walked around the next morning on a tour of the account, they were showing me around each of the areas. We got to one area, and they said, "This is where we are examining claims that are rejected by the computer system, and we have to have an examiner make the determination of the validity of the claim."

I asked how many claims went straight through system and were either paid or rejected without going to a manual claims examiner; the answer was less than 5 percent. That was the systemic issue. That was what needed to be corrected and fast. That was why the claims payments were backlogged and also why EDS was losing so much money on this account.

I had seen claims-examination areas previously, and they are quiet rooms with professionals sitting at computer terminals, looking at information, carefully making determinations, and entering the answers. Just about everyone in this room was standing, walking around, and talking with each other. Almost nobody was sitting at a computer terminal and typing. You could tell that no work was getting done.

I walked over and listened in on some of the conversations. It was quickly apparent that very few of the examiners knew what they were doing. Every time they pulled up a claim, they had to walk around asking other examiners if they knew what to do. There were very few experienced people in the room, and each of them had a line of people waiting to talk to them

"Where are the experienced claims examiners?"

"They are teaching the new hires."

"How many people are in this room."

"One hundred fifty."

"How many new hires are in classes now?"

"Approximately two hundred fifty people." Note that this was in addition to the other four hundred fifty people on the account.

"How many experienced examiners are tied up teaching these classes?"

"About fifteen experienced claims examiners."

"Why are you hiring so many new examiners?"

"We are behind and trying to catch up. We need a lot more people to adjudicate the claims. Once these people graduate from class, we will have around six hundred fifty people on this account. We have a plan to move to a larger office to house them."

I appreciated that they were trying to do something, but his was the exact wrong thing to do. Hiring so many new people would just recreate more rooms like this one with a bunch of rookies asking questions and nothing getting done. We needed to get the computer system more automated so we did not need so many examiners, and until we could get that going, we needed experienced examiners sitting quietly at screens, accepting or rejecting claims. That would get the money flowing to the hospitals and to EDS as well. They were trying to solve the problems with manpower, but that would take months to show an effect. You can't kill every problem with manpower.

In talking with them, I determined that we had about twenty-five well-experienced claims examiners. They were all either teaching or answering questions from the rookies. We had to get those few experienced claims examiners on a computer system and adjudicating claims. And we needed to do that fast.

By lunchtime that second day, we had our first big recovery plan:

- We were going to terminate all two hundred fifty people who were in training, unless they were already an experienced claims examiner.
- We were going to terminate all of the rookies in the examination rooms.
- We were going to sit the twenty-five experienced claims examiners down and have them adjudicate some claims.

These moves would shed costs, would get payments going to hospitals and doctors, and would make a big cut in the losses on the account's P&L (Profit and Loss Statement). That was fast progress that would be noticed.

When I told the account manager what we were going to do, he was incredulous. He had talked with his manager by now and knew that I was legitimately in charge. After we discussed it, he said that he saw the logic in it. So he and his group started working to implement this—today!

On that second afternoon, I had some big figures to give Ross on the daily call. He was happy.

Now, I know terminating so many people was harsh. So was bankrupting the hospitals and doctors in this state. That would have denied health-care access to millions of people. Sometimes, you have to make difficult choices, so make the right ones.

The afternoon of that second day and the morning of the third day were spent in talking with the analysts and the people in the EDS systems engineer development program about why claims were being rejected by the computer system and sent to human examiners. We printed a list in rank order of the reasons for rejection. We went to the top of the list, and I asked if we could prioritize our requests to the programmers for modifications to the systems to bring this one to the top of the list. This account had previously submitted 532 requests for modifications to the computer systems, and the poor programmers (or developers as we call them today) were working very hard on making all of these changes. We decided to cancel 527 of these requests to give them some relief and to leave five important requests that automated the top five reasons for rejecting claims. We told the developers, "Just focus on getting these five improvements done as soon as possible."

The developers were stunned, and we had to have several conference calls with them to explain the abrupt change in requests and what we were doing on a business basis. After they understood, they dove in and started to make things happen. We saw progress every day.

Later that first week, the first computer system change took effect on the fourth ranked reason for rejections. That change took our percentage of claims flying through the system without human intervention from under 5 percent to over 10 percent. Things were starting to happen.

Four months later, this account was caught up-to-date in processing claims for the state. Hospitals and doctors had seen a huge increase in payments. The governor was happy, and he called Ross to say so.

The account was down to 117 people. On the EDS P&L, it had gone from losing half of the company's profits to increasing the company's profits by 15 percent that year.

There are two big leadership lessons to take away from this story:

1. When you are in crisis, start doing something quickly.
2. When you have a big problem, make sure you start working the systemic issue that will most affect the overall solu-

tion as soon as possible. Ignore all of the flotsam and jetsam in the waters and focus on solving the systemic issues first.

In crisis situations, many people will be trying many things to solve the crisis. As a leader, you need to figure out what is most important and focus people on that. You need to gain their confidence and help them get organized and working. You cannot let panic consume you. You have to be calm and in charge, and you have to do the important and systemic things first.

Figure out what to do quickly. Get some action plans going. Focus on the most important items and drive them to a solution. Lead your team to success. Then, you can all celebrate together.

By the way, the account manager in this story turned around and was an enthusiastic and knowledgeable partner in getting this account working better. He deserved credit for the turnaround, and I made sure that he got it. He continued to have a long and successful career at EDS. He was a good guy.

Information Technology Icon: Glen Self

Glen Self is one of the smartest business people I have known in my career. He is also one of the most unusual ones—very effective, but totally and completely surprising and regularly outlandish and weird.

Glen has a PhD degree in operations research, a highly mathematical disciple of decision making. He was on the faculty of Texas A&M University when he was recruited by Mort Meyerson to join EDS as a vice president. For years, he worked there with only three people on his professional staff; all three had PhDs in operations research from Texas A&M where Glen was their supervising professor.

Glen was the ultimate troubleshooter for EDS. When any project went off the rails, or any account was not making enough money, or any customer was unhappy, and after many people

---

tried to correct the situation, Glen was called in, and he solved the problem. He or one of his teams dove in, found out the critical issues, and pushed all parties to a successful resolution.

After years doing troubleshooting, Glen added additional business units—opening new industry verticals for EDS (like public utilities). He also added a group to monitor and encourage EDS in adopting new technologies.

After I worked in the public utilities group for Glen, he asked me to move to Dallas to join his group of troubleshooters. I was a young person, still in my twenties, and I did not have a PhD in operations research like all the other people in Glen's group at that time, but he wanted me. I enthusiastically joined, and that started one of my most intensive learning periods. I was exposed to accounts and business efforts all over the world and got to lead engagements to change things quickly. Glen was challenging and aggressive to those outside of his group, but he was challenging and supportive to those in his group. As long as you were doing great work, Glen was happy with you. He led so many important turnarounds for EDS and was one of their most valuable officers.

Glen Self had a fundamental distrust of bureaucracy; he always lined up with the person in the field on the job near the customer and lined up against the corporate staff people at the headquarters. I've heard people in the field organization call the growing staff members at headquarters "revenue-sucking pigs," and this is how Glen saw them. He saw business in terms of right and wrong, never in terms of how it followed the corporate-recommended processes.

One of the more humorous incidents I saw Glen do was when he was about to be given a gift for ten years of service at EDS. Glen objected to such gifts, saying that they were a waste of company money. He said that the company should reward people for the value they brought to the company, not how long they hung around. But he lost that argument, and EDS adopted a policy of giving people a desk clock noting their ten years of good service.

Glen knew that Ross Perot hand-delivered the clocks for ten years of service and that the time was near when Ross would come by his office to deliver the clock. A few days before his tenth year at EDS, Glen brought in a large fish aquarium and filled it with water in his office—no fish, no filtration system, no rocks or decoration, just an, otherwise, empty aquarium filled with tap water. Glen refused to tell us why he had the aquarium in his office.

On the day of Glen's tenth year at EDS, Ross came into Glen's office with a box wrapped nicely with the clock inside. Ross said some nice things about Glen and, then, handed Glen the box. Glen took the box and put it to his ear, saying, "It's ticking. It could be a bomb. We can disarm it by submerging it in water." He, then, dropped the box into the aquarium.

All of us, including Ross, were stunned. That was very disrespectful of the gift, but as we thought of it, it was classical Glen—being absolutely unbending in participating in any wasteful corporate process. Ross just shook his head, laughed, and said with a smile on his face that he was glad that Glen enjoyed the gift and found a use for it.

Another example was when I was working at EDS to staff a new project. Ross hated bureaucrats and considered a human resources department dangerous overhead (remember that the HR department at IBM installed the sales commission plan with a cap on earnings that led Ross to leave that company). So you had to network to staff a project with company insiders, and if you were not a leader known for taking care of your team, then, you could not staff a project. There is a certain rightness there.

I found an EDS person in our Washington, D.C. office who fit the needs of my project and who wanted to join me. He asked his current manager who said this person was key to the work there and that he could not release him to me for six months. I told Glen this. Now, remember, this is when EDS ran under "jungle rules," as has been described earlier in this book. Glen told me to tell the EDS employee to resign and that we would hire him the next day at a higher salary. This kind of behavior would get you fired immediately in most companies, but there was a certain efficiency in getting the rarest resources to the places where they would make the most positive impact for the company. It is chaos, but it does work. Just don't do this in other organizations.

The leadership principle that you should learn from Glen Self is not to be disruptive to the rules of an organization but to be mindful of what is right, no matter what the rules are. Glen's method of looking hard to find what is right is the method you should learn. Only if you *know* what is right can you operate to get the organization to *do* what is right. You have to see through all of the processes to the direct view of right and wrong. Then, you can work to get the company to move to that destination.

Encourage continuous learning—game films

When I was at Perot Systems, Mort Meyerson hired a very talented leader to help us with corporate communications and teaching leadership—Robert A. Wilson. Bob Wilson was a very talented man who had grown up in New England (and carried the Boston accent the rest of his life) and, like many others, had moved to Texas and fell in love with the mythology, romance, enthusiasm, and relentlessness of it. Bob had excelled in a number of jobs, one of which was as CEO of the public broadcasting station in Dallas, where he was the first to bring *Monty Python's Flying Circus* to the United States. Bob's family was also incredibly talented; his wife, Laura, is a renowned photographer, and his sons, Andrew, Luke, and Owen are all successful in the movie business.

Bob brought a creative idea to one of Mort's leadership meetings. He said that in professional football, there is not much learning during a game; the real learning happens on Monday, in the film room where the game is dissected play by play in slow motion. That is where you see who missed the block which allowed the other team to tackle the quarterback, for example. Bob said he would like to bring this concept into business and would like to make films that our company could use to help people learn. He said the most intensive learning occurs when you fail rather than when you succeed, so he wanted to film us right after we had a failure and to capture those lessons for everyone in the company.

The group enthusiastically endorsed this idea; we were all ready to see it happen. Then, Bob asked the tough question, "Which of you are ready to have me film you when you fail?" No hands were raised. Everyone looked at everyone else or averted their eyes from Bob. Bob was undeterred and told us to think about it and talk to him when we had something appropriate to film.

Nothing happened for months. Nobody volunteered to be filmed when they failed. Then, I was leading a chase for a huge piece of new business as head of sales and marketing. Europcar had been a customer for a few years. We had outsourced their information technology function and delivered a new rental-car reservations system for them. Europcar was half owned by Accor, a French hotel company, and half by Volkswagen, a German automobile manufacturer. They were affiliated with National Rental Car in the United States. National was looking to outsource their IT function as well, and the winner of that would also be in the driver's seat to also outsource Europcar once our existing contract expired. So we had the opportunity to gain a big new client—National—and to cement an existing business relationship—Europcar—for the long term. The decision to outsource National would be made by the National team, but that would be very heavily influenced by the leaders of Accor and Volkswagen, based on their experiences with outsourcing at Europcar.

The two finalists were Perot Systems and EDS, both companies that had been started by Ross Perot. Many people at Perot Systems was working on this opportunity from our CEO, Mort Meyerson, down. We had teams working to convince National to decide for us and, simultaneously, teams working to optimize our relationship with Europcar to get their executives on board and supportive. The executives of Europcar saw this (correctly!) as an opportunity to renegotiate our contract in their favor. So we were renegotiating with them and selling National, all at the same time. Many of the senior leaders of Perot Systems were involved in this effort.

As the decision came down, we successfully renegotiated our contract with Europcar and got their enthusiastic support for us at National. We presented our bid to National and were selected as the winner, but almost immediately, EDS reduced their price significantly (we heard almost 30 percent) and bid to do the work for National at below our costs, so we did not respond. We had an almost all-night session negotiating with Europcar that we closed, but then, we heard that the decision from National in the United States was to do business with EDS, and we had lost.

We were all physically and emotionally crushed. We had led hundreds of our team for months in this chase, and we had lost. Not only did we lose National, but that meant that these two linked companies would highly likely consolidate their IT operations, and we would lose Europcar in the future. It was an overwhelming defeat.

Bob Wilson had been working with us, and I called him the next morning after we had lost and asked if this would be a good candidate for his game films idea. He enthusiastically agreed and immediately asked me to get every one of the key players to fly to Dallas the next day to be interviewed. We were all exhausted but agreed to give this a try.

When each of us arrived, Bob put us in a conference room with a video camera on us, and he interviewed us. He asked a number of questions about the sales effort—what happened, what else could we have done, why did we lose, how did we feel about it, etc. He got us to talk openly and brutally honestly.

We did not know until later, but Bob had the camera focused on our face much like Mike Wallace of *60 Minutes* would do when he was interviewing a crook or a swindler. His camera was on a close-up of your face, and it showed every line, every grimace, every sigh. Then, Bob went to work editing the film.

When I saw the finished product, I was stunned at the graphic realism and the emotion that came across in the film. I looked like I was exhausted, and someone had beaten me into within an inch of my life. I never thought I could look that bad. Everyone else looked beaten as well. The images were powerful.

The words we said and the advice that we had were almost all the same. We regretted that we had not worked hard enough; we regretted things that we thought were unimportant, so we ignored them, and they bit us; we took responsibility for the loss personally and did not blame anyone else; and most powerfully, we said we would never ever let ourselves or our company get in such a losing position again. You could see the rock-hard resolve going forward from this loss and that we learned some lessons that would make us stronger.

When Bob showed the final film to other employees of Perot Systems, they were blown away by the honesty and openness of the leaders who admitted failure, and they were enthused about being in a company that could deal so openly about a loss and was so committed to be better in the future. The film was very powerful. It showed specific lessons, but more importantly, it showed a company culture of continuous learning. It showed that even very experienced executives could still learn and grow. What a powerful lesson.

Bob was right. There was learning in failure, and he showed us the way to extend our learning to others in our company.

This is a powerful story, but the ending is even better. After EDS quoted the low price, they tried to recapture margin during the contract negotiations with National. These were tough negotiations, and after sixty days of negotiating, National gave up on ever getting the service and price they thought they were promised, so they called us back at Perot Systems. We got a contract signed in less than thirty days and had a very positive experience with National and Europcar for years in the future. What a nice story!

The leadership points are to never stop learning and to let your team see you as capable of learning. That is powerful for the long term.

Learn new ways to handle business disputes

When I was at Perot Systems and running our business in Europe, I learned a number of cultural lessons that helped me be a stronger leader and also a leader with a broader skill set. A broader skill set can always help you.

We had a dispute with one of our customers in Germany. They were not paying us, and we had been unable to get the CEO to agree to pay, even though we continued to provide services, and he wanted us to continue to provide them. We were at the point where in the United States, we would call in the legal team and file a lawsuit to collect our fee.

One of the members of the Perot Systems board of directors was Carl Hahn, the former chairman of the management board and CEO of Volkswagen AG. Herr Doktur Hahn was a very experienced international businessman and a very smart person. He was always available to help us when we asked.

I met with Carl, told him the situation with this customer, and told him my plan to pursue a lawsuit to settle the dispute. He said, "No, no, that is not the way that we do things in Germany." I asked how we should settle this dispute. He said, "Let me look up the board members of the customer." He did and found that he knew one of them. In Germany, the boards of their large industrial companies are made up of business leaders who, many times, know and respect each other. Carl said here is how we should settle this dispute:

1. You tell me your side of the story and what you want to happen in a settlement.
2. I will call the board member of the customer and set up a dinner with him.
3. He will ask the CEO of his company to tell him their side of the story and what they want to happen.
4. The two of us will have a cordial dinner and negotiate a fair agreement to settle this dispute.
5. Then, we will each come back to the two company leaders and inform them of the resolution and what they should do.

I was astounded. This was straightforward and could work quickly; we could settle something in a week that, if we went to court, could take years to conclude. But could it get settled like this? I signed on to give it a try.

Dr. Hahn had his dinner, and the next morning we met. I was amazed at his grasp of the important details. He told me of their discussion and their recommendation. I would say that we got about 90 percent of what we wanted. This would have been an overwhelming victory had it come from a court order. But was the other company satisfied? Carl said yes, and later, I talked with the CEO, and he was happy. He paid us, we continued working, and we had a close and happy relationship for years afterward.

This incident showed me that there are different ways to settle disputes, and calmly laying out the dispute and the positions could result in a solid agreement. Once you removed the emotion from the dispute, it was easy to get an agreement.

I like the German system rather than our litigious practices in the United States. It is much more efficient and effective.

IT Industry Insights
Two Methods of Product Pricing

The new technology adoption cycle has several consistent patterns, and one of the most important ones is that prices and margins decrease over time for products. Sometimes, the price increases nominally but with additional capabilities added for that price; in other words, the price/performance delivered to the customer was better.

For illustrative purposes, let's take a systems management software product and trace the steps of the price over time in order to show the two primary ways that you can work to maintain as much margin as possible over time.

Phase I. One company, many times a start-up entrepreneurial company, comes up with some software that makes operating data centers far easier and/or far more efficient. As they are the only source for such capabilities, they have an opportunity to

---

value price; that is, they can charge less than the value that product brings to a customer. That, typically, allows the customer to save substantial money and the vendor to make a great margin.

Phase II. As other competitors develop similar capabilities, the price for that product starts to decrease. Rather than value pricing, vendors have to respond to the competitive prices in the market to sell. The price starts to decrease toward the cost of developing it versus the value that it brings to a customer. Cost-based pricing does not deliver exciting margins for vendors.

Phase III. Assume that multiple vendors have an overall systems management software product and that they are going to add this new capability into the suite that they sell as their base product. Now, there are two very different pricing approaches to use:

- *Incremental pricing approach.* The vendor can charge separately ("a la carte") for the new capability. This allows the vendor to obtain new revenue for that capability which delivers more value for customers. Now, the vendor's base product will be under price pressure from competitors, so the vendor can decrease the price of their base product over time, realizing new revenue from the new capabilities for which they charge separately. This is one method to maintain good margins over time.

- *Maintain base price approach.* The vendor can decide that they will add this new capability to their base product and leave the price of that base product the same. In one way, they are giving the new capability for free, but what they are really doing is maintaining the price of their base product over time by adding additional value to it. This means they will be premium-priced for their base product versus their competitors, but they will claim to deliver more value to match that premium price.

Sometimes, vendors use both of these approaches. If the new capability is something that most of their customers would value, they may add the capability to their base product and use it to maintain the price of their base product over time. If the new capability is something that only a few customers would value, then charging for it incrementally makes the best sense.

Pricing is tough in the IT industry because of the massive competitive environment in almost all segments. Knowing what you are trying to do by pricing is important because you have to work very hard to maintain prices and margins over time. That is how you build a successful IT business.

Have the broadest view of creating value

When you are a CEO, your job is to make the company more valuable, treat the customers well, and develop the team members. You have to take the broadest possible view of how you can do this. Having that broad overall view is one thing that makes CEOs different. They look at every little issue with the perspective of the broad view of how the solutions affect the entire company—all of the customers and all of the team members. CEOs learn this lesson quickly, or they fail.

Also, once you are a CEO and learn to think broadly like this, you always think that way. Even if you take a job as a division manager, you still think broadly for the good of the overall company. You cannot go back. This does make you a more valuable employee, even if you are not the CEO.

My wife, Susan, had been a vice president and had responsibility for a thousand or more people in a large company. When she was about to accept a job as CEO of a very small company, I told her that job was tougher than her prior VP job and that it would change her forever. She did not believe me on either count, but after a few years as CEO, she agreed with me. She adopted that broad view, and it was a far tougher job than she expected. But she thinks like a CEO to this day and always puts the broad company interest first. As a former CEO, I knew she would experience that transformation.

To illustrate the broad view that you must have as a leader, let me recount the time when I and others failed to have that broad view and the potential loss in value that occurred.

When EDS first started, the information technology industry was in its infancy. The processing machine of choice was a mainframe computer. Large companies purchased them, primarily to perform back-office functions faster, more accurately, and cheaper. Most companies that had mainframes ran them at a maximum of around 50 percent efficiency; in other words, they only used half of the processing power that they bought. EDS pioneered the outsourcing concept, and they developed software tools so that they could run the largest mainframes at 92 percent efficiency or better. So they could go to a company that had a midrange computer running at, say, 50 percent efficiency and move that load to their large mainframes that had better price/performance *and* were running at 92 percent efficiency. This created a lot of value. EDS could charge the company less for computing than they were paying and could also make a nice profit on the outsourced account. Their software and expertise were creating great business value.

At this time, there were no systems management companies or tools like IBM Tivoli, HP OpenView, CA Unicenter, VMware's vSphere, and others. EDS was the only game in town, and they reserved their software for their outsourced clients to build their business.

Over time, independent systems management software companies like the above did develop, and they sold software tools to companies which allowed them to run computers at a similar level of efficiency as EDS. So these software companies captured the value that EDS had in its original business proposition. And they created valuable companies.

Services companies—like outsourcing companies—today have a value of one times revenue. Software companies have a value of five to ten times revenue. A reason is that software companies can grow faster, and they are far more profitable than outsourcing companies.

Far more valuable companies were created in the systems management space than EDS.

So back to the broad view. EDS had excellent systems management software a decade earlier than did the systems management companies, but EDS only used it to support their outsourcing business. They did not take the broad view that they could have created a systems management company and owned that space. Their business model blinded them to the opportunity that they could have created far more value with a different business model of a software company, in addition to their outsourcing company.

Think broadly—whether you are a CEO or a leader anywhere in the organization. Don't accept the past history of what your company did and did not do as the boundaries on your thinking. Try to look at your assets and the opportunities in the market to see how you can craft the most value. Be creative. Be bold. Make it happen. Lead!

IT Industry Insights
Services Commoditize Over Time

There are a number of patterns in our industry, and one that you need to understand is how technology solutions move through the industry and customer bases. As this cycle repeats over time, it disrupts the business models that are most appropriate and the margins of each. Understanding the pattern will allow you to take advantage of the cycle at whatever type of company you are currently working.

Let's take an easily understood example of the merging of the analog telecommunications technology with the digital information technology that occurred in the '80s and '90s. At Advanced Telemarketing (ATC), we were the first in the call-center industry to connect an analog-automated call distributor to a digital IT system. This was important to us as we were answering calls from multiple catalog companies, and if we could connect these two disparate

---

technology systems, we could deliver a call to the ear of a sales representative at the same time that we delivered a screen to their computer system, containing the script and information from the catalog based on the toll-free number the customer had dialed. This is a no brainer today, and everyone does similar things, but let's trace the path that this technology took in its adoption cycle.

Phase I. Leading large companies and services companies see the opportunity and craft a solution to obtain substantial benefits. ATC was able to merge the groups of representatives answering each catalog company's calls into one large group and gain significant cost savings by consolidation. IT services companies saw this opportunity and started to take this to market to help other large companies employ similar technology. These were million-dollar services engagements that delivered significant benefits to the customers and great margins for the services company. Systems integration solutions like these are the mainstay of many services companies. They are always on the lookout for opportunities to find new, high-impact solutions like these.

Phase II. Other services companies enter the market. Once competition starts, the margins for the services companies start to drop. The engagements are just as valuable for the customer; however, once you make it a process to deliver these integrated solutions, the time and cost required to deliver, then, decrease. So they deliver less top-line revenue for the services companies as well as tighter margins as competition takes effect.

Phase III. Hardware vendors see the opportunity to add functionality to deliver these benefits. From both the telecom and the IT side, the vendors see the opportunity to add adjacent capabilities to their products which will make them more appealing to customers, and for which they can charge additional fees, so they make it much easier to do these integrations. This pretty much kills off the nice opportunities for the services companies.

Phase IV. Every vendor delivers this functionality. Once this capability becomes a significant competitive differentiator for a vendor, their competitors add the same capability. Instead of a technology differentiator, it then becomes table stakes. Also, the opportunity to charge additional fees goes away, and the base price for the vendors' products includes this capability. To close on our example, with VoIP technology today, you cannot imagine that it was a difficult task to synchronize the delivery of a call and a screen to a representative. Everyone includes this as a feature.

In four steps, this valuable capability for customers goes from high-margin, million-dollar services engagements to free capabilities in every vendors' products. The cycle repeats. This cycle has driven productivity improvements in industry, profits for well-positioned vendors, and challenging tasks for technologists. Knowing the cycle will allow you to know where you are on the opportunities for good margins and when it is time to fold your cards and just include the capability for little additional charge.

Forming teams—get everyone in the right positions

There are considerable differences in leading a large organization and in leading a start-up company. One of the more subtle ones is in the talents of people and how you form them into teams with each person playing certain positions.

As you advance in leadership in large companies, you see less and less new hires. Most of the people in your team will have been with the company for some time. They will have been in different positions and, sometimes, are new to your group, but they are experienced. They have also been tested and have performed well in other jobs at lower levels. So your team has been filtered, and many of the people who do not fit in have been weeded out at lower levels.

Therefore, the challenge is to get the organization right and to get the right people in the right slots. Look at the business challenges you have and form your team to meet those challenges. Don't be afraid to change the organization but make sure it is appropriate for the task.

When I did troubleshooting jobs in large organizations, I saw a lot of groups that were absolutely not performing and were failing miserably. What I repeatedly found, however, is that there were mostly good people in these groups; they were just doing the wrong things. They were not evil or untalented people; it was just that their view of what the company needed was wrong, and the messages and incentives set by their leaders were wrong.

People under pressure tend to put blinders on themselves and their teams. They tend to give out orders to focus their team on doing what they think are the most important tasks. They lose sight of what they are doing for the entire company by only thinking of how they can be successful on the task in front of them. The lose creativity and adaptability while they try to muscle results over the line.

Earlier, I talked about an example at EDS when a health-care account was very backlogged in processing claims. They saw that business issue, and their plan to cure it was to hire more people. What they missed was that their processes and systems were so poor that it would have taken a cast of thousands to solve their problem with people. What they needed to do was focus on the systems and processes, get those right, and then, scale the people as necessary.

It is hard under pressure to keep this broad business view. And it is equally hard to not think that your people are letting you down. You can get down on them easily.

In large enterprises, make sure you focus on the broad business issue and get that right; then, get the people in the right positions. That is the way to success.

In small start-up-type organizations, almost everyone in the company is a new hire. You hire a lot of strangers, and you make a lot of mistakes in doing so. You don't have the years of filtering helping you in building competent teams like you do at higher levels in large organizations.

Therefore, the challenge in start-up organizations is different. You have to get people formed in a team to succeed, but many of your people are not whole and complete business people; they have great skills, but they also have great weaknesses. The emotional maturity of the people in entrepreneurial companies is far lower than in large organizations due to the lack of filtering, but you still have to get the work done.

Instead of thinking of the ideal organization like you would in a large company, you need to think about what organization can get the work done now. Once you hire more people, you can move toward the ideal organization, but it is usually done in a series of steps. You reorganize more frequently in smaller organizations.

In one smaller company, I had a challenge in that the company was not growing. Sales were not going well. The sales team was composed of people with deep industry knowledge, that is why they were able to develop the breakthrough product that they were taking to market. But none of them had ever been in or led sales organizations. They did not understand the sales process. I had to hire an experienced IT sales person who had zero industry knowledge to couple with the industry experts I already had to make a whole and complete sales organization. As the experienced sales leaders learned the industry and product, I could move the industry-knowledgeable people back to product-leadership-type jobs. The one industry-knowledgeable person who could learn sales processes stayed in sales and was a success. So my organization was a pairing of an experienced sales person and an industry-knowledgeable person. That was inefficient, but it was quickly effective. Over the long term, I moved back to a more traditional organization with much greater efficiency. Task one was to be effective—to close sales. Task two was to be efficient—to close sales at a reasonable sales cost. To succeed, you had to do the tasks in that order.

I've joked that if you want to lead a start-up, you have to mold a team of a one-legged person, with a blind person, with a one-armed person to make a full and successful team. This is, obviously, a silly analogy, but it does bring up the real point that you will not have whole and complete performers in a small company, but you still have to be successful. The pressure is on the leader to support people so that they can exercise their strengths while their weaknesses will not be revealed. You have to work both sides—their strengths and weaknesses. Be attentive to both when you are designing your organization.

IT Industry Insights
Diversity of Thought and Experience

We all hear about the power of diversity in forming teams, and that is powerful. Let's talk about one element of diversity in how people think and what prior experiences they bring to their current role. It is essential that you form teams in your organization that will have such diversity; otherwise, you are highly likely to under-perform other teams who have such assets.

There are various methods to measure how people think. One of the more widely known ones is the Myers-Briggs test which categorizes people on the following four scales:

- Extraversion/introversion
- Sensing/intuition
- Thinking/feeling
- Judging/perceiving

At Perot Systems, we did not have great diversity of thought and experience. A lot of our team members had very similar backgrounds—military, technical education, formerly at EDS, etc. To illustrate this at one of our leaders' meetings of the top one hundred leaders, Mort Meyerson brought in someone to administer the personality and thinking tests, and then, divided us up into four groups of like-thinkers to solve a problem. It was very funny watching how the groups of like-thinkers handled the problem. You could see superficial aspects just by watching the action in the four corners of the room where the groups had gathered:

- The Type *A* aggressive behavior group was, by far, the largest, probably two-thirds of the entire leaders' group.

That group stood in one corner of the room, pretty much shouted at each other, came to a consensus on solving the assigned problem in about twenty minutes (even though we had been given an hour to do so), elected a spokesman to report later on the solution, declared victory, then adjourned and went to the bar.

- The consensus group first decided to clear out their corner of the room and form chairs in a circle so they could all be seated and discuss the issue. The hilarious thing that I observed was that they had each brought more than just a chair for themselves, so the circle had far more chairs in it than were needed. They had a vibrant discussion for the entire hour and asked for more time. They could not come to a consensus or a recommendation.

- The analytical group asked for some white boards to display facts and data. They asked the facilitator for more information. They were paralyzed because they thought they did not have enough information to come to a solid decision.

What we saw by this exercise is that having all like thinkers in a group causes lots of negative issues. For example, the Type A group flew over the issues at a high level and developed some very simple and not thought-through recommendations. Other groups were not even functional enough to complete the assignment.

When you form teams, try to get the best mix of thinking patterns so that you will have robust examinations of the issues to develop comprehensive and workable solutions. That is the great decision-making that you need to build great companies, and it starts with building a leadership team that brings this diversity to their job.

Establish optimal communications for teams

At Pivot3, we reached a point in late 2016 where we were seeing some communication and alignment issues cropping up in our team. When we were a small, entrepreneurial company, it had been easy to keep everyone focused and aligned. We had just exceeded two hundred team members, and while the misalignment events were few, they were very frustrating and were something that had not happened previously.

We began to think about what had changed and what we could do to get back into the close alignment that lets smaller organizations work so much more efficiently and effectively than larger organizations. We found some very interesting academic studies about groups by anthropologists looking at teams. Anthropology was, obviously, not the place that a new fast-growing technology company first looks for ideas, but in this case, it was very helpful and important to our future growth and success.

Anthropologists had studied human behavior and teams over the course of history and found a significant commonality with many groups such as:

- Hunter-gatherer societies
- Amish in the United States today
- The *Domesday Book* of residents of eighteenth-century England
- Hutterites in Monrovia in the sixteenth century
- Roman legions
- And now, technology start-up companies

When you look at the above list, it is very challenging to see what the commonality is among them. The answer is that all of these groups have been shown to be able to establish stable societies and act in an aligned way, until they get to a size of more than one hundred fifty people. Above that size, they tend to break down, separate, and go their own way into two distinct less-than-one-hundred-fifty-person groups. The lesson is that with less than one hundred fifty people on a team, you can have informal and one-to-one communications which suffices to keep the group stable and aligned. Once you get larger than one hundred fifty people, you either have to split into two independent teams, or you need to start using more formal communication mechanisms in order to keep your group aligned.

This one-hundred-fifty-person number is one of those "magic" numbers like the 80/20 rule that we all hear quoted so often—you know, 20 percent of the customers provide 80 percent of the revenue; 20 percent of the employees provide 80 percent of the technology and intellectual property breakthroughs, etc. In fact, this one-hundred-fifty-person maximum team size for informal communications is called Dunbar's number.

When your company or division gets larger than one hundred fifty team members, you need to start layering in more formal communications methods to keep alignment. Even in a larger organization, if you are leading a team of more than one hundred fifty people, you need to use some additional communication methods. Fortunately, today, with electronic communications so available and so cheap, this is easy to do, but you cannot avoid doing it if you want to keep your team aligned, productive, and effective in achieving their goals.

At Pivot3, our senior leaders developed several new communications mechanisms which we implemented beginning early in 2017. Michele Fanning, our VP of communications and Bruce Milne, our VP of marketing, led us in these efforts, and they were quickly effective. They not only minimized the misalignment issues, they also gave a new burst of team spirit and knowledge of the overall company to every one of our team members. It was amazing how quickly these communications methods became part of our culture. It showed us that we were doing something right when we adopted them.

Below, I've laid out the things we adopted at Pivot3 for you to use as a guide. All will not necessarily fit your team, and you may need additional ones, but this should be a good starting point for you and your leaders to develop their communications plan *before* your team gets to having more than one hundred fifty people.

Pivot3 company communications plan. We moved aggressively at Pivot3 and simultaneously established several formal communications mechanisms to help us better align our team which was exceeding the two-hundred-person team size. Below are the mechanisms that we adopted:

- *Annual company meeting.* We started 2017 with an all-hands company meeting of several hours long. This was an in-person meeting at our largest office and a video conference meeting elsewhere in the company. At the company meeting, we reviewed our progress from the last year, talked about our successes and failures, and then, we laid out the plan for the upcoming year. We also had a session on major product introductions. Two of the more popular things we did were the Above & Beyond Awards and the Senior Leader Question & Answer time.
  - o *Above & Beyond Awards.* We decided to recognize individual performer team members who had literally gone above and beyond what we expected to serve a customer, to invent a new product, to supercharge a partner, to help others in the company, etc. There were three criteria to be eligible for these awards: (1) the person nominated had to be an individual performer, not a leader; (2) the person had to be well-respected in doing their regular job; and (3) the person had to go significantly out of their way to do something even more important for the company. We took nominations from anyone on our team for these awards, and then, we selected the best of the best to be the winners of the Above & Beyond Awards. The Above & Beyond Award winners were talented, creative, intense, and relentless. That is what made them such winners. These awards became more popular each year, and the stories we got to tell everyone in the company were even more impressive in future years.

o   *Senior leader question and answer session.* This part of the company meeting was always ranked as the most interesting. Prior to the meeting, we solicited questions from everyone in the company about anything they wanted to ask to one of the senior leaders. We, then, grouped them into themes. To make this session more interactive, Michele and I saw the questions prior to the session but we did not tell the other senior leaders. We just put them up on stage during the webinar broadcast and fired away with questions to them. Most of the questions were very good and were addressing either opportunities or issues within the company. The senior leaders got to talk about a lot of important things and seeing them interact with the audience and with each other was a big hit.

- *Monthly fireside chats.* I like to read history, so I was familiar with the positive impact that US president, Franklin D. Roosevelt, made via his radio-based fireside chats when he talked directly to our citizens during the Great Depression. At Pivot3, we started a fireside chat as a monthly event delivered by video conference to all of our team members worldwide, then recorded and posted on an internal site for viewing later. This was a chance for me, as the CEO, to talk directly with our team since we worked to make these interactive, not just as a broadcast. We allowed team members to submit questions prior to the webinar and also to ask them during the webinar. For an introverted CEO who likes all of their communications to be scripted, this would not work well, but for me, as an extrovert, it was effective and fun. I talked on certain subjects and, then, brought in guest speakers of other leaders to talk to our team about their area as well. We tried to do a minimum of updates and a maximum of perspective setting. One of the advantages you have as a CEO is that you have the broadest view of the company versus other team members who only see their particular area. It is important to share that broad view with the entire team so that they can use that broad perspective in doing their job better. These fireside chats were a big hit with our team members, and one that they invariably talked about with candidates we were recruiting to join our team. Telling them that they can hear the CEO talk and even ask questions to him every month was a big deal and a differentiator for us versus other companies. This also allowed us to keep all of our team members focused on our most important initiatives. It made us more agile and more responsive to both opportunities and issues.

- *Pivot3 Idea Exchange.* We formed a group of individual performers, elected by their peers in each functional area, to meet monthly with the CEO and, sometimes, another senior leader. Their term would be one year with two face-to-face meetings and ten video conference meetings that year. The first time we did this, there was some trepidation from people about surfacing opportunities or issues to the CEO. After a few meetings, the team members saw that this was an effective way to get issues, which were most commonly cross-departmental process issues, raised to a higher level so that they could be solved. We let team members self-nominate to be a member of the idea exchange, and then, each functional area elected their representative from among the nominees. This was a very effective group in improving the operations of the company. In a big vote of confidence in how this group worked, the second year we did the idea exchange election, more than two-thirds of our team members nominated themselves to be a member of this group. That was very cool.

- *Leaders' meeting.* In addition to our weekly senior leader executive staff meeting, we added a monthly larger meeting to keep the next level of leaders up-to-date on important corporate initiatives. This was a great way for us to hear from a broad swath of talented people talking about the key initiatives in the company.

- *Win-o-grams.* We began announcing key sales and recognizing the team, then expanded this to include accomplishments from team members in other areas. These were brief emails just to say we did something well and to recognize the key people who made it happen. Having a steady stream of wins coming from the CEO allowed everyone to stay updated and absolutely built the enthusiasm for our joint accomplishments.

- *Newsletter.* To reduce the clutter of email announcements, we grouped less critical ones into a monthly online newsletter.

- *New team member orientation.* We changed our new employee orientation to focus on culture and people rather than just the administrative processes of being a team member. This was important because in a fast-growing company, you can lose the culture that made you successful if you do not actively work to preserve it. When a new employee reported, they got an orientation from our HR team and their leader. Then, after they had been with us a couple of months, we brought them in for a group orientation led by senior leaders, which talked about culture and process. One of the most insightful comments I heard after this session was from a team member who told me, "I have been here about six weeks and seen that Pivot3 operates differently than other companies. It is very open and aggressive about fixing problems and moving fast. It has a very healthy culture that respects and values each team member. I thought this culture just happened to develop, but after hearing you talk about the culture we want in the company, I now understand that you leaders designed this culture and did the hard work to make sure it worked like you wanted. That has made this a great place to work." What a great compliment. At this session, we talked specifically about good and bad cultures in companies. See the Industry Insight section for a list of the topics we discussed.

- *Team member survey.* Our final communication thrust was to institute an annual team member survey. There were some rating questions, but most of them were open-ended ones that allowed people to comment; e.g., "What are we doing well in ___ area?" "What do we need to improve in ___ area?" I read every one of these comments as did our other senior leaders, and they gave us a huge amount of information about things we needed to improve or to do more of. Also, giving an honest summary of this survey to every team member earned us credit for transparency and helped us get everyone involved in improving the company.

A big part of effective leadership is communications, so do not fail to address this professionally and formally when your team gets to that magic size of more than one hundred fifty. It is very important and a responsibility of a leader to make sure these communications are working.

Ron with the Pivot3 team in the United Arab Emirates

IT Industry Insights: Defining and Propagating a Winning Culture

One thing we did at Pivot3 in our employee orientation sessions was to contrast the behaviors that one sees in large companies versus the behaviors that allow smaller, entrepreneurial companies to win. The following slide lists the behaviors that we discussed with our new employees since many of them came directly from large companies.

Behaviors That Win

Big Company	Entrepreneurial Company
• Annual budgets	• Tactical spending – very frugal
• Cover all markets globally	• Win big in a few markets
• Overwhelming support & materials	• Enough support to win
• Personal view: your department	• Personal view: the whole company
• Focus: internal to company	• Focus: external from company
• Get a promotion to advance	• Build the company larger under you to advance
• Compensation on your performance	• Wealth creation on company valuation
• Play defense – blame game, hiding	• Play offense – win, swarming
• Sub-optimized – playing to advance incrementally on multiple fronts	• Optimized for massive overall growth
• Many teams, many agendas	• One team, one agenda

Pivot3

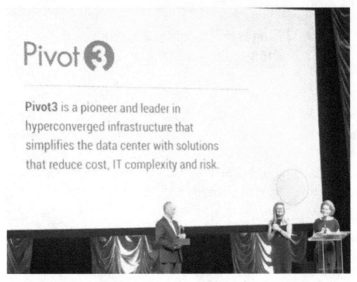

Ron accepting the A-List Award for Austin
start-up companies in 2017

Reengineering processes is the journey, not the destination

As leaders, we have to recognize where our company or our area is in its development cycle. When the company is small, it is very easy for everyone to help it work efficiently. As it grows, people begin to specialize, and everyone does not have the same information base; therefore, problems in processes continue to crop up. These process breaks and/or inefficient processes will drag the performance of the company, so they have to be cleaned up.

Processes are the way that the company works. Generally, processes enable the company to work most efficiently. That is certainly the goal. In a few cases, processes, themselves, can be a differentiator for the company. One of the best examples of this is Dell where Michael Dell and team designed the most efficient supply chain processes in the IT industry, thereby giving themselves price and delivery time advantages over their competitors. Moving your processes to be the best in your segment is a minimum goal for you to have.

We all see problems crop up in our companies. When they do, you need to work on the following two levels:

1. You need to correct the error. Dive in, take charge, find out the problem, and solve it quickly. One of Ross Perot's many pithy sayings was, "When you see a snake in the office, don't call a committee to analyze what to do, don't convene a big meeting, don't call a snake consultant for advice, don't survey industry best snake-killing practices; just pick up a stick and kill the snake!" That is the right intensity to have in cleaning up errors. At Pivot3, we called this swarming. In a healthy company culture, people from all around the issue gather together to pitch in to solve the problem quickly. In an unhealthy company culture, people run from problems, saying, "Not my responsibility," and point fingers at each other. But the first step is to have resources swarm to clean up that individual problem and do it fast.

2. But swarming is not enough. Once you have solved that individual issue or cleaned up that individual transaction, you have to analyze back to the root cause of why this problem occurred. When you do this, you usually will find some process errors or missing pieces which allow the problem to occur. Now, you have to get the cross-functional team together to reengineer the process so that this problem will not occur again. Many companies call these cross-functional meetings, interlock sessions. You need to make sure that you work these interlock issues with the same intensity as you swarmed to correct the first instance of the problem. Don't let them drag on. If you are swarming over and over again on correcting the same issue, you may be performing, but you are not correcting the root cause. You need to do this. In the military, these are called after-action reports. It is important to see a problem and, then, plug the holes in your processes so that it does not repeatedly occur.

I have one final recommendation for you on cleaning up process issues. You need to work these intensely and relentlessly. It is not enough to say you are working on cleaning up the process; you have to do it and complete it. I've seen too many people who want to make a career of "working on" a process. They like going to meetings and like working with people outside of their own area. Such activity is as destructive as political activity in your organization. Make working these interlock issues important, not prestigious. It is not a destination to work on a process; it is a journey to make your processes tight, effective, and efficient. Just get it done and get it done quickly.

No game-time coaching

I learned a great leadership lesson at a seminar led by Randall Stutman of CRA. He is an executive coach who has helped many corporate executives become better leaders. One of his clients was Mike Krzyzewski, the very successful basketball coach of Duke University. Mike is a great leadership coach himself. Let me pass along one lesson that Randall taught him.

Randall observed that during a basketball game when there was a timeout, the coach got to talk to the players. Sometimes, the advice was on a play to run or on a way to defense the other team. Those suggestions immediately helped the team. But significantly, he noticed that, at times, the coach gave specific personal advice to one player, such as, "You are lowering your elbow when you shoot a jump shot. Raise your elbow, and it will help you score." In these circumstances, the advice was almost always counterproductive. The player started focusing on his elbow, not on making the shot. He questioned his mechanics and lost the confidence to make shots. The time to correct mechanics is in practice, not during the game. You need to keep the confidence up of the players during the game.

So Randall's leadership lesson is no game-time coaching. Leave the players on the field alone to do their best. Coordinate them but don't try to change them during the game.

I saw this played out on a TV game during the March Madness tournament last year. Duke was behind at the end of the game, and one of the players made a last-minute shot to win the game for them. After the game, the TV host interviewed the player and asked him what Coach K said to him in the huddle. The player said he diagramed the play and, then, looked at him and said, "You were made for this moment!" That confidence played out in him making the shot to win the game.

At Pivot3, we were late in the quarter, and in order to make our sales goals, we had to close on one large opportunity. Our leaders were on the phone with the sales leader giving him a lot of advice. Once they had finished, I summarized by saying, "Mike, you are our best, and there is nobody I would rather have on this challenge than you. Just go and do what you do best."

After that comment, I heard a sigh from the sales leader. The relief that he felt and the confidence that he was gaining was palpable. He went out and closed that deal, and we made our goal for the quarter. Practice your team relentlessly, but no game-time coaching.

Protect your team during a financial crisis

My grandfather, Henry D. Nash, worked for the Western Electric Company. This was the famous company that produced the telephone and electrical products for AT&T and the Bell System of regional telephone companies in the United States. Telephone services was a monopoly in the United States and in other countries until deregulation opened the US market in a series of steps in the 1980s.

Henry was an electronics technician for Western Electric (this is where the nerd gene comes into my family) and was a member of the unionized workforce at Western Electric. I can remember reading the union newsletter which he received when I was spending the night as a child at my grandparents' home.

We were talking one day about business and his career, and I asked the open-ended question of what things were like during the

Great Depression of the 1920s and '30s for him and for his family. He started talking about it and, then, said something that I thought was so important. He said that Western Electric made the decision to not lay off people but to reduce salaries instead. That is, instead of laying off 10 percent of their workers, they would cut everyone's salary by 10 percent, which essentially generates the same cost reductions for the company but keeps the entire workforce and productive capability intact. He said they did a number of these salary reduction rounds. I asked what percent of his original salary he was receiving at the nadir of these reductions. His answer, "Fifteen percent!"

I was amazed and asked how he could possibly live on only 15 percent of his original salary. He said it was possible and that he was blessed. "I was the only person in our neighborhood and one of the very few people I knew who had a job every day of the Depression," he said. He continued, "With the significant deflation that occurred, prices were reduced, and everything was cheaper. I was able to pay the mortgage and keep our house. We were able to buy clothes for the kids and, with our garden in the backyard, were able to put food on the table. We never missed a meal. We considered our family as one of the luckiest and most blessed during that time."

Wow, that was a strong statement of the priorities from the sole breadwinner for a family—a roof over their heads, clothes on their backs, and food on the table. Those priorities stayed with me but so did the idea of broad-based salary reductions rather than layoffs.

Decades later, I was an investor as a partner in a venture capital fund, InterWest Partners, headquartered on the famous Sand Hill Road in Menlo Park, California. In 2008 and 2009, we had a global depression triggered, in part, by overinvestment and overvaluation of the real estate sector and under-capitalization of financial institutions. It was scary for everyone and life-changing for many. This was clearly the most serious depression in the United States since the 1930s. For everyone working at that time, they will always remember what effect it had on business and what they did to survive.

As a board member of a number of venture-capital-supported startup firms during that time, I participated in many board discussions of how each company could react in order to best assure its survival. Significant layoffs—soon and in large numbers—were clearly advised by most board members. I remembered my grandfather's experience in the Great Depression and the reaction of Western Electric where he worked. I brought up his experience and asked those firms to consider broad salary reductions rather than significant layoffs. The risk was that their key employees might leave for a better-paying job, but this was a slight risk during a depression where few firms were prospering and hiring new workers. The gain could be massive in that they could retain all of their current employees and be better-staffed than their competitors. This could accelerate their relative position with their competitors and, when the depression ended, could propel them into a segment leadership position.

I was not successful in convincing any of the companies to try this salary reduction and full employment model other than one—Vendavo. Vendavo invented software which allowed companies with extensive product offerings to adjust prices in an automated way, customer by customer, and based on actual experience, to increase their revenue and also to retain more of their customers. Customer retention and vendor revenue growth might seem to be counter to each other, but they were not.

Vendavo business leaders made the decision to reduce salaries by the following scheme:

- Employees making under one hundred thousand dollars annually were not subject to salary reductions.
- Non-officers making more than one hundred thousand dollars had their salaries reduced by 10 percent.
- Officers had their salaries reduced by 20 percent.

These salary reductions would stay in place until the company returned to profitability. At that time, one-half of the earned profitability would go toward restoring the salaries to their original levels. In addition to this salary-reduction scheme, the employees who had salaries reduced were issued additional options to purchase stock of the company. That could reward them as the company became more valuable.

The result of these actions was that during this tough couple of years, Vendavo, with its entire staff in place, surged ahead of its competitors in the segment. Once the slowing of the economy started to wane, Vendavo started to accelerate its growth. It came out of the depression with a motivated staff and great momentum in the market. The CEO of Vendavo at that time, Al Crites, deserved credit for listening to these ideas, implementing them in the appropriate way, and holding the confidence of the employees of Vendavo during this scary economic time.

But the idea came from my grandfather. A long-ago idea adapted for current times. That is another form of leadership. Having a knowledge of business history can help you be a better leader in current times. My advice to business leaders is to not neglect what companies have done in the past; don't copy it either. The big win is when you can gain ideas and adapt them to your current challenges and opportunities.

A related topic is the assumption that a hot economy lifts all companies, and a slow economy hits all companies. This is absolutely not true. My experience at EDS and Perot Systems, both outsourcing companies, was opposite to this. At both of those companies, we did well, and our growth was most steady in very hot economies or very cold economies. We struggled to grow in flat economic growth times where things had been steady for years.

The reason for this phenomenon is that the process of outsourcing—that is, turning over certain functions of your business and a number of your employees to an outside company—is a very difficult decision for business leaders to make. It is difficult to admit that outsiders can do a better job than you can with your own team. So when the economy was very hot, executives were willing to consider outsourcing because they were seeing that their team could just not keep up with the growth, and this was limiting the company's overall growth. So they made that difficult decision to outsource. At the other end of the economic spectrum, when the economy was very cold, they were willing to consider outsourcing because they had to cut costs to help their company survive. Difficult decisions can be prompted by desperation. That is the simplest lesson to learn.

The more complex lesson to learn is to have the dispassionate discipline to make difficult decisions no matter what the overall economic pressures. As a business leader, you should always be looking for a way to improve your organization. Don't just want until you are in desperate straits; put the pressure on yourself to improve each and every day.

InterWest Partners' Texas office partners—
Berry Cash, John Adler and Ron Nash

Ethical behavior has to be beyond reproach

One area where there can be no compromises if you want to be a leader is in your ethics and how you conduct yourself. The absolute minimum standard is to be completely ethical in your actions, plus in the appearance of your actions. Nothing else is sufficient.

You are in control of your own actions; you know that. But you also need to be in control of how you are appearing to act. You cannot let yourself get put into compromising-looking ethical situations. A leader is always on and always visible. Remember this and avoid even any appearance of an ethical flaw.

I hate to spend much time on this point because you probably already know it, but it is an absolute deal-breaker for your career as a leader if you fail an ethical test. It demolishes the trust that your team and others have in you and makes it impossible to continue to progress.

Ross Perot was very aware of this requirement, and he emphasized it in an extremely direct way to his leaders and his team. Ross said the following to the officers reporting to him and also said the same thing in multiple company meetings, "If you find someone in your group who has done something clearly ethically wrong, like stealing money or cheating a customer, I do not want you to fire them. I want you to fly them to Dallas and bring them into my office. I want to have the fun of firing them!"

That is certainly an in-your-face statement, but it gives the clearest statement of the requirement for ethical behavior in your company, with your customers, with your partners, etc. Do not test the boundaries of ethical behavior; always stay in the center of the road. That is the only way to continue as a leader.

Establish Faith as the foundation

Talking about religion in a business context is risky since our organizations consist of many people of many different faiths. However, I cannot write about how I developed my leadership skills without talking about the important factor that religious faith plays in my life.

I am a Christian. My faith forms the foundation of everything that I do. I could not do what I do without the presence of Jesus Christ in my life. He carries me every day. I was blessed by having parents who took me to church and brought me to religion as an important part of my life.

I would encourage you to check out Christianity if you are not a person of faith or if you are looking for an anchor to your life. However, I understand that many excellent leaders come from different faiths. There is just not one way to be a good business leader, but I would contend that a faith-based servant leadership model is the best one for long-term success. You can see that over and over again as you look at successful leaders.

I have seen that two institutions change people's lives the most—education and religion. Every business leader knows the importance of education, and many of them benefit from fine educations. I had a great engineering education at Georgia Tech and a great business education at the University of Texas at Dallas. Every business leader should know the benefits of faith. Faith can improve your life and the lives of those around you. Faith is as important or even more important than education in your business success. So give faith its due and focus on it, as well as educating yourself. And, join a church or religious organization as that will help you grow in your faith as my church, Highland Park United Methodist, helps me.

Take time to figure out how you want to live your life. Take time to investigate and learn about faith. My recommendation is that you adopt the Christian faith as the foundation for your business life, as well as your personal life. You can also benefit from other faiths in your business career. But please do not ignore the power of God in making you a better person and a better leader. It works. Take it from me; it does.

4

Drive Yourself to Produce

Once you are learning the skills of leadership, you enter into the next level of learning. How can you drive yourself to larger successes as a leader? That will require intensity, effort, relentlessness, perseverance, and stamina. Leaders who continue to rise are ones who push themselves to improve every day. You cannot teach that intensity; it all comes from a commitment to do it and from an internal strength which gives you the stamina to focus on getting better as a leader, each and every day. Great leaders carry this intensity for their entire lives. That is one way that they separate themselves from others.

If you are not early, you are late

As I have said, my father and mother shared so many characteristics. They were driven to succeed and relentlessly focused on success each and every minute. Mother was the one who drove the children. She was an absolute maniac about certain things such as doing your homework early, never waiting to near the deadline to start. She was also a maniac about being on time for every event. "If you are not early, then, you are late. And you never ever want to be late." Those were great leadership lessons.

I cannot tell you how many times we were early for events and ended up standing around waiting for them to start. At church each

Sunday, the minister parked in the first parking place nearest the sanctuary. The Nash family generally parked in the second place. On our slowest days, we parked in the third place. We were never late.

I made very good grades in school. I loved school, and I loved to learn. But I was not always ready to jump on long-term assignments immediately. That caused great consternation and conflict with my mother because she wanted me to start working on every term paper the minute after it was assigned. I was normally not a big procrastinator, but I did like to let things slide for a while like most children do. We regularly butted heads, and she regularly won.

I mentioned the EDS systems engineer development program earlier and talked about the second phase of that program as being classroom instruction on computer architecture and programming held in Dallas. This was another very competitive event at EDS and a lot of people washed out of the class. I was determined to succeed, and I remembered my mother's lessons of starting immediately. The multiple-months-long course had five individual problems which they assigned. Essentially, these were all specifications to develop a computer system; they started with a basic system and got progressively more challenging.

Late one afternoon, they assigned the first problem to our class. After they explained it, they said they were giving us two days to get this project done and turned in for evaluation. My classmates all got the assignment and then talked about going to dinner, then back to their apartments, then to come in the next day to work on this project, which seemed to be relatively easy to do. They asked me to go to dinner with them. I declined. I had another plan.

I stayed in the office by myself and immediately started on the project. I wanted to complete it as soon as possible. I wrote the software and got the system partially working sometime after midnight and finally finished at 4:30 a.m. I went to my apartment, showered, shaved, and was back in the office by 8:00 a.m. As my classmates were all sitting down to start working on the project, I walked up to the instructor and turned in my project. He was amazed, and they were amazed. I got it entirely right and received a grade of 10 out of

10 for it. But more importantly, I established a pattern of early success which is so important in business.

I used the same strategy for the next four problems. I did not get them all done in one night, but I did pull an all-nighter to start every one of them. By the last project, about half of our class was spending the all-nighters with me. I was the first to finish each project and got the maximum grade for all five projects. But I did something far more valuable; I showed that I was willing to push aggressively to reach business goals, and I established myself as a leader. When they ranked people in our class upon completing the class, I was ranked #1 by all three of our instructors. Mother's leadership lesson worked.

By the way, this is when I picked up the nickname, "Flash Nash," due to my being first over the line with all of these projects. It was a great nickname and a good one for a leader.

I learned another important business leadership lesson during this class. One of our classmates had an MS in computer science. We all considered him to be the smartest person in our class. When they assigned that first project, he disappeared to his apartment and did not return until the afternoon, after the project was due in the morning. He turned in his project, and it ran perfectly the first time. We were amazed. The rest of us had all needed multiple test runs to get it right.

But our instructor was not amazed. He counseled that student. He said when you have business deadlines, you need to meet the deadlines. Missing the deadline was not good, no matter how well you thought you had done. He encouraged him to not be such a perfectionist and to stay in the office and work with others to get his work done on time.

This person did not take that advice. On the second problem, he was one day late. On the third problem, he was two days late. Then, he got fired.

Our instructor talked with us about this issue. It is hard for some to understand that it is not how smart you are but how much work you get done by the deadline that is most important. As a leader, performing is of utmost importance; you have to lead a team to make deadlines. We all felt sorry for the guy who was fired and asked couldn't the company use him somewhere else. The answer was no; this was a business, and if you were unwilling to react to business issues, you were not a valuable employee.

EDS was an aggressive and, sometimes, harsh environment, but it had a lot of very smart people that were absolutely determined to succeed. Ross Perot established that ethos and lived it each minute of every day. Every company cannot adopt this model, but they can learn from it. As a leader, you need to stay out front and on top of your game. If you do not show the winning attitude, neither will most of your organization. Like they say in the infantry, "Lead from the front."

Be relentless—produce every day

One of Ross Perot's favorite quotes is from Winston Churchill:

> "Never give in, never give in, never, never, never, never—in nothing, great or small, large or petty—never give in."

Ross used this over and over again in talks with employees, and he exemplified the relentless nature that this quote inspires. As I wrote about in an earlier section of this book, Ross showed this intensity every day. As detailed earlier in this book, when I was given the assignment to turn around the operations of one of our failing accounts, Ross had me call him every afternoon at 5:30 p.m. to tell him what I accomplished that day that made our company more profitable. I did this every day for four months. You can imagine the backbone and steeliness that this imparts to a young employee.

In all my assignments since then, I had tried to lead teams with the same intensity. I have told multiple groups that one of my favorite words is "relentless" and that I want our company to be known by that term. It is a strong leadership lesson, and Winston Churchill's quote is a great example of the relentless nature that you need to succeed.

A business lesson that a lot of new employees do not know is that total production counts. At one of my start-up companies, Pivot3, we had a team member who had the benefit of a great college education—a top undergraduate school and an MBA from a top business school. He was very smart. Once, we promoted another person, and this team member came over to talk with me. His position was that he was smarter than the other person, and he should have been promoted first. I understood that thinking from someone right after college.

But the business reasoning was different. I told him that he was smarter than the other person. But he came in at 9:00 a.m. and left before 5:00 p.m. because he had an appointment with a personal trainer at 5:30 p.m. every day. The team member we promoted was in early and worked late. He produced more. I said, "This is not like college and taking a test to see who is the smartest. This is a business that needs production from all team members. We judge contribution by the quality and the quantity of production from each team member. That other person produces more than you and is a better role model. That person can be a good leader someday. You need to think about your priorities, and if you want to be promoted, put a higher priority on business. You can succeed here if you make the commitment."

You need to be relentless in trying to produce as much as possible. You need to produce every day. That is how you get ahead and how you get to earn leadership opportunities.

Relentless—Ron making a business phone call while on the roof of a centuries old building in Jeddah, Saudi Arabia

Information Technology Icon: Ross Perot

Ross Perot's story is well known—growing up in the small town of Texarkana, Texas, attending the United States Naval Academy, becoming the top sales person at IBM, founding EDS and later selling it to General Motors, founding Perot Systems and later selling it to Dell, and running for president against Bill Clinton and George H. W. Bush. Ross was patriotic and very supportive of our military. He was engaged in innumerable civic projects, usually anonymously, and he raised a great family.

I benefited by working for and with Ross at EDS and at Perot Systems. He had great faith in individuals who stand up to big organizations and do the right thing. I learned a lot of leadership lessons from him.

Ross's leadership style is characterized by intensity, directness, relentlessness, and activity. Problems rarely get better with age, and confronting them directly and quickly is almost always the best method. Ross showed a singular nature of fearlessness in confronting a problem. Ross ran at 100 miles an hour every day; there was not a moderate bone in his body; he was always on, always intense, and always focused.

As an example of this nature, he called me one morning, saying that he had heard that one of our larger health-care clients was upset with our service quality and had a problem with it. I had heard that from our health-care leaders who were in the process of preparing a recovery plan to present to me. I told Ross that we were working on a recovery plan to get the situation turned around quickly. That was not fast enough for Ross. He said, "Ron, that customer is headquartered in Dallas, call their CEO and get us an appointment to meet him today to hear his view and talk about solving this problem." As usual, Ross would not slow down for the rest of the team to catch up. I called and found that the CEO was in an all-day session with his senior leaders. Ross saw that as perfect. I got permission for Ross and I to come into that senior leaders' meeting to listen to all of them.

We got in the car, drove over to the customer, and barged into their leadership meeting. Their people there were awestruck at seeing Ross Perot in person and very deferential to him. Ross started the discussion by asking what was wrong and what we could do better. The CEO and leaders were very open about listing out the deficiencies of our service and had some good suggestions on how to mitigate them. I ended up with three pages of notes and comments. We left the meeting with the leaders of our customer absolutely convinced that we were being responsive to their issues, serious about solving the problems, and working with intensity on making improvements. Their anger and frustration with our team was totally diffused, and the business relationship with us was even closer. I had a list of things to get done, and it gave me the information to drive our team to the right priorities as quickly as possible.

So many people shy away from direct communications on difficult issues. This example shows the power of confronting problems directly, forcefully, and quickly. That was part of the essence of Ross Perot's leadership style. He was fearless and went directly at the solution; no guile, no trickiness, no spinning, and very little planning—just fervent activity. That's direct action and the path that Ross advocates in confronting issues. In the infantry there is an axiom that if you are lost or confused during a battle, that you should "run toward the sound of gunfire" to get reengaged. That's great advice in business also—run toward problems, not away from them.

This is a key leadership principle that you should learn and use in your career. Don't ever be scared to confront issues directly. You will get a huge amount of credit for listening, and you will learn a lot by doing the listening yourself, not delegating it to staff members.

Ron, Ross Perot, and Susan Nash in New York the evening prior to the Perot Systems IPO on the New York Stock Exchange—big smiles all around

Do volunteer work—it's important!

If you are a hard-charging person and push yourself to create a great career, then, you will find yourself regularly under stress. You will need relief from that stress from time to time, and how you relieve stress will also be a big part of your career growth. There are a host of unproductive ways to relieve stress like turning to alcohol, drugs, dangerous sexual behavior, or abusive behavior. These will tank your career. Don't use risky and unhealthy ways to relieve stress.

Let me talk about a very productive way to relieve stress that worked for me for decades and where I also learned additional lessons about leadership—doing volunteer work. One of the most recuperative ways to relieve stress and to increase your self-esteem is taking the time to volunteer to help others.

One time, I found myself late in the afternoon of a business day in pretty low spirits. Things had not gone well that day, and neither my company nor I had been successful. It had been a frustrating day, and I was tired physically and emotionally. I just wanted to go home, curl up in the fetal position, and get some rest. So I decided to leave early. I checked my calendar for the rest of the day and found a big problem—I had committed to go to my children's school to a board committee meeting that evening. I was exhausted; I was stressed out. How could I do that? Maybe, I could just skip the meeting; would they really notice? I decided since I was the chairman of the committee, I had to attend. I hated it, but I had to force myself to attend.

I drove to the school in a daze; I was driving on autopilot. When I got there, the first thing I noticed was that the staff person from the school had prepared the room for the meeting and laid out the handouts. She greeted me very enthusiastically and was thrilled that I was there to help them. Then, the other committee members came into the room. They were excited about the meeting as we had important things to do. They were highly motivated to meet and make some decisions. They were enthusiastic. I opened the meeting, and we got into it—lots of discussion, give and take, insights, and comments. We worked hard for several hours. We made progress, made some decisions, and produced some good results.

At 9:30 p.m., we started leaving the meeting, and everyone was congratulating each other for the great work. They also congratulated me for leading them in doing so. It was fun. It was rewarding. I drove home feeling energized, proud, satisfied, etc.

In summary, at 5:30 p.m., I was defeated and exhausted. After several hours of volunteer work, at 9:30 p.m. that same day, I was energized and confident. The volunteer work absolutely healed me and made me stronger. That is a productive way to relieve stress. That is a great way to restore your self-esteem.

In addition, you learn a lot about leadership in volunteer organizations. Think about it; in business, you can hire and fire, you can give bonuses or raises. Those are great ways to motivate people. In a volunteer organization, you have the same leadership challenges, but you cannot give someone a raise or hire a new person; you have to deal with the volunteers you have. You have to get the job done, but you have less tools to motivate people than you do in the business world. This will stretch you and allow you to learn leadership lessons.

In fact, the leadership tools you use in volunteer organizations are better tools to use in business than raises and terminations. They are basic motivational skills which you need to use in business also.

So get involved in your community in a volunteer organization that speaks to your passion. It will refresh you from your business stress, and it will improve your leadership skills. This is important for your long-term career success.

Ron doing volunteer work in China repairing
the Great Wall with the VMware team

Laying a wreath on the Tomb of the Unknown
Soldier with a volunteer organization

Find your work/life balance

Establishing a balance between your working life and your personal life is a topic which is regularly discussed in the media and in general business discussions. There are millions of people who are trying different methods to get this right. I've listened to many people talking about this, and my view is just different from most of them. This is a very important point because if you get this wrong in one direction, you will break down personally, as will your family life. If you get it wrong in the other direction, your career will not develop and grow at the rate you expect.

To show my thinking on this subject, let me give you some background. I made good grades in school and was generally considered one of the smarter students. I graduated from a good university, earning an engineering degree from Georgia Tech. After Tech, I went in the army for a couple of years and, like a lot of people, was recruited by Ross Perot's EDS from there. My first assignment was at an investment banking company on Wall Street in New York City which Ross owned.

When I started, I was young, and I was in excellent physical shape from being in the army and being in the infantry which is the most physically demanding part of the army. I had a high energy level, and I knew how to push myself. Infantry training was designed to induce stress so that you could learn how much you could push yourself without breaking. I learned that I could do far more than I thought and could operate for days on little food or sleep. The point is that I was in great shape, was aggressive, and was ambitious to make my mark in the business world.

My thinking as I started at EDS went along these lines:

- I think that I am smarter than the average person, but let's just assume that I am not.
- If the average person works eight hours a day, that sets the benchmark.
- If I could work ten hours a day, at the end of a year, I would have produced 25 percent more than the average person.
- If I could work twelve hours a day, at the end of a year, I would have produced 50 percent more than the average person.
- These were significant figures, and ones that would propel my career to a fast start.
- Now, if I were smarter than the average person, I would be even farther ahead, but at a minimum, I knew I could outwork other people.

Some people may cringe at thinking like this, but when do you want to push yourself in getting your career accelerated; when you are young and healthy with few family responsibilities or when you are in your forties with a lot of other responsibilities? I chose doing it when I was young (now, I will admit that I never really stopped working long hours, but that is another story, and one that shows me to be the zealot that I am).

I immediately got known for working long hours and was positively recognized for it. Since my first job in Phase I of the SED program at EDS was to cover some customer areas, I got to work before anyone in that department did and was the last one to leave each day. People notice things like that.

I took over from another SED who was leaving to go to Dallas for the computer-science training portion of that program. He told me what he did each day, and I was stunned by it. He had been trained by a prior SED to do this each day. Someone had talked to the customer, and they requested a new report to be produced each day. This person, rather than going through the process of getting approval for a new report to be generated automatically, went to one of the developers and got him to program a "one-timer" to produce the report. In those days, the nightly job stream was run off a set of punched cards rather than systems management software that we use today. So each day, this SED went to the data entry area and punched up a set of cards; they, then, went to the people controlling the nightly job stream and asked to insert these cards in the test cycle which the developers used to test their programs against actual customer data. The cards would cause that program to run the next night. In the morning, you had to go over to the area where the printers were for the developers and find that report. Then, you could hand-deliver that report to the customer.

Now, this did work, but it was several hours of clerical work each day, just to get one report. I asked around and learned how to get this to be an approved job and report. It took me about a week to get it all set up. From that point forward, the job ran automatically and was delivered to the customer along with the other daily reports. That freed me up from about five hours of running around each day.

I told my manager what I had done and that I had freed up most of my day. I asked him what else I could do to help the company with the time I had created. Two days later, I got called to meet the overall account manager who had heard what this new employee had done. He was effusive about complimenting me and gave me more authority on the spot. I, now, led three SEDs in one of the areas.

I kept working smart and also working hard. In a couple of months, the two investment banking companies that Ross Perot owned were planning to merge. As part of that transaction, they consolidated the teams to work on the merger tasks. Based on my good work and my long hours, I gained responsibility for all one hundred fifty SED program members at the two banks and got to lead that team through the merger of two companies. This was a lot of responsibility for a new employee, and it taught me a lot about making mergers of companies successful. I had been an employee for only a couple of months and was now leading a group of one hundred fifty of my peers. But I knew how I earned that opportunity—through lots of good work.

This just shows how quickly you can distinguish yourself if you are committed to finding important things to do to help the business. Think like you own the business and try to make it more valuable. Take some initiative and make something happen.

Now, rather than just talking about the work/life balance that is heavy on the work side and works well for a person, let's talk about the potential costs. Mort Meyerson was a key leader at EDS and ultimately was president of the company. After Ross Perot started his second company—Perot Systems—and decided to run for president of the United States, he asked Mort to come into Perot Systems as CEO and Mort accepted. By this time, Mort was executing his transformation from an aggressive, combative business leader to a broader, more balanced leadership model—Mort 2.0 as I called it earlier in this book.

Mort made an observation that he regularly talked about to the team at Perot Systems. He recalled that in the early days of EDS, there were about twenty people who were appointed as vice presidents. They were all in their late twenties or early thirties. These people were all like Mort 1.0 and worked intensely, many times to the detriment of other parts of their life. Mort observed that if you define failure as death, divorce, drug addiction, nervous breakdown, complete exhaustion, or forced early retirement, half of these young VPs had faced personal failure by the time they were fifty years old. In almost any business process, a failure rate of half would be absolutely unacceptable. There had to be a better way to advance your career. Mort asked insightfully, "Do you have to be miserable to create wealth?"

The answer is no, you do not have to be miserable, and there are better ways to build a career and wealth. Mort 2.0 wanted to lead with these ways in mind at Perot Systems. He became a different and better leader.

I was able to build my career as well as other parts of my life, simultaneously. I conscientiously worked to make sure that even though I was working long hours at the office, I was also intensely focused on the other phases of my life. An easy illustration is that I focused on my children as intently as I did my work. They will tell you that and also tell you that, sometimes, it was a bit too intense for their liking. As an example of that intensity, when my son was a senior in high school and one of the captains of the football team, I was primarily working in Europe. Each Friday, I got up very early in London and took the early flight from there to Dallas, arriving in the afternoon. I attended each of his Friday night football games finishing up just before midnight in the US. That meant that I was up and moving for twenty-four hours straight. That is a long day but it was important for me to be in the stands and watching all of those games. I knew that and was doing my work/life balance—just in my own relentless way.

Getting work/life balance right is important. But think about work/life balance not as an everyday metric but over the course of your long career. When you are young and without kids, put in the hours and get ahead. In the middle part of your career, prioritize your family and make them a success. Once you are an empty nester, you can go back to pushing on your career. Do this, and you will have the assets to fund a great retirement. Leave the office every day at 5:00 p.m., and you will be working for a long time just to feed yourself.

The Mary Kay cosmetics company in Dallas that was so successful used to have a mantra for their employees; "God, family, Mary Kay!" Those were the priorities that allowed you to have a sustainable and successful career. Get this balance right, and it will serve you well.

Discover healthy stress relievers

I have observed that many hard-charging business leaders have an unusual way of relieving stress—they add on more stress. I learned this lesson when I was running a start-up company under very adverse financial conditions. The stress was massive and even when I went home, I still thought about business. I thought about my problems all weekend. It was always in my mind.

Then, I started racing sailboats. Now, most people think racing sailboats is very stressful, and it is. You are competing and trying to beat the other boats, skippers, and crews. But what I learned is that racing a sail boat is a challenge in optimizing multiple metrics—your crew performance, choices on which side of the lake on a windward leg, proper sail choice and shape, steering to pick up on every gust, etc. When you are leading a team and steering the boat, your mind is absolutely focused on the race, and nothing else can enter your thinking during the intense period of a race.

I found that I enjoyed racing sailboats and that after a Saturday of racing in a regatta, I was absolutely tired but also relaxed and clear-headed. The intensity of racing had allowed me to escape my worries about my company. I had not been able to think about business problems for a day. It had cleared my mind and reset my thinking. At the end of the day, I was tired and happy to have a burger with my crew while we told stories about the race that day to learn how we could be better in the next race.

I needed a hobby of that intensity to provide the stress relief from my business. It sounds counterintuitive, but it is true; some people need intensity to get relief from other stresses. I have known CEOs who race cars, which is also intense. Others compete in marathons. The point is to find out how you can positively relieve stress and do it. That will help sustain the edge that you need to succeed. Leaders figure out this individually; just make sure the stress relief is positive and not self-destructive.

Information Technology Icon: Jim Cannavino

Jim Cannavino's path to be one of the top executives at IBM was the most unusual of any leaders who obtained that level of success. He came from a family with poor economic assets. He married and had a child while in high school and had to go to work to support them; he never attended college. He started at IBM as a repairperson and—by the sheer power of his brain and his hard work—rose to be one of their most senior officers and the top internal candidate for CEO in one of their searches.

As a footnote, Jim's reputation is stellar but suspect by one group, as he was one of a string of IBM executives who, in negotiating with Bill Gates of Microsoft in the early days of the personal computer industry, failed to grasp the economic sea change of value moving to the operating system and applications versus the computer hardware. These IBM executives allowed Microsoft to capture most of the value of their business relationship and to build a giant company. They missed a great business opportunity for IBM.

Jim came into Perot Systems as president, along with Mort Meyerson as chairman and CEO. Jim had worked for IBM for more than three decades, so his experience was vastly different than most of the people at Perot Systems, but he knew how to scale organizations, and that is what we needed. I learned a lot from Jim about how to scale large organizations. Those were important lessons.

Jim Cannavino had one of the more unusual patterns of work/life balance that I have seen in my career. He would typically work for several weeks at an intensive pace.

- Working a twelve- or fourteen-hour day, beginning with a breakfast meeting, continuing through the business day, and concluding with a business dinner.
- Working this pace for seven days a week over the course of six weeks or so.

At the end of one of these cycles, Jim would disappear to his house on the ocean for a week or ten days. He would spend time on his boat, relax, and decompress. He would be available for a few business calls and did respond to some business emails but only to important issues. He used the time away to recharge his physical and mental stamina.

Then, Jim would come back in town to the office and start the next cycle of intensive work. I would not recommend this as a good pattern for most people, but it does point out the need for executives to take time away from work. None of us can work day after day, effectively, without any breaks.

The leadership lesson we can learn from Jim Cannavino is to find a pattern of work and time away which works for your company and for you as an individual. A career is a marathon, and you have to have the strength and stamina to continue to race. Find out an acceptable pattern and make sure you don't allow yourself to be overstressed, exhausted, and run down. None of us are at our best when we are exhausted.

5

Focus on Developing Others

Once you get proficient at being a good leader yourself, you have to focus on continuing to learn in order to progress. The next level is to make a commitment to others much in the same way that you made a commitment to becoming a great leader yourself. Unless you are invested and absolutely committed to developing your team members, you will top out as a leader very early. Great leaders develop great teams. That is how they succeed. You have to focus on others to develop great teams. Be more intense on helping them succeed than you are on helping yourself to succeed. That will make all of the difference.

One verse from the Bible that points this out is from Mark 9:35, "If any man desire to be first, the same shall be last of all, and servant of all." If you are building a team, then, you have to focus on helping that team succeed. That is the best way for the business to succeed and for you to succeed as a leader. If, as a leader, you show ambition to your own career over others, everyone on the team will pick that up and will not be as strong of a team member as they could be if you led them as a servant leader.

You now know that the focus has to be on helping others. Let's look at some ways that you can do that.

Build a personal relationship before doing business together

My grandfather, Henry D. Nash, was born in the Kirkwood area on the east side of Atlanta. It was an area of small wooden-frame houses in the early 1900s when he was born. Using today's economic strata, we could call the area middle class or lower-middle class. It was a safe, positive place in which to grow up. His father was a car salesman, so he was in the business of seeing new people each and every day. I did not know my great-grandfather but imagined what he was like having known his son—my grandfather—well.

Papa—as I called my grandfather—was good with people. He had a great network of friends and was constantly expanding it. When I would go with him on a Saturday morning as he was running errands, I noticed that every time he went to a shop, he spent time talking with the people working there about personal things before he talked about why he came to the shop. Whether he was getting a TV repaired or buying a tool at the hardware store, he first talked to a person at the store. I asked him once why he did this. He said, "You always want to build a personal relationship with a person before you do business with him. That way, you know that you have a friend working for you, not a stranger who does not care for you. And that person knows he is working for a friend as well. It makes a huge difference in the service level you get."

Wow. I thought his friendliness was just how he was; that was true, but it was also a deliberate method of getting superior service. That made a big impression on me. My grandfather whom I thought was just naturally gregarious had worked to be that way. I wanted to be like that, and his comment motivated me and gave me confidence to be that way. I needed to work on that skill. When I met someone, I first needed to get to know them, personally, then talk about why I was there. That was a valuable lesson.

You might think this was just a cynical ploy to butter up people to get better service. If you carry that high level of cynicism, that is all you will learn from this lesson. But if you lower your level of cynicism, then, you can generalize from this lesson that the best way to build lasting relationships with people is to work on the personal relationship, as well as the business relationship. This is the powerful leadership lesson that I took from my grandfather. If you have a genuine personal interest in people on your team, for example, that will lead to much healthier and more robust business relationships than if you don't really care about your people personally. Even worse is to fake a caring because once people see through that, and they will, they will turn on you.

I realized value from this lesson in the 1990s when I was at Perot Systems. I picked up responsibility for leading our operations in Europe. I had done business around the world earlier in my career, but this was going to be an immersion in multicultural business. Our largest account in Europe, Europcar, was in deep trouble with our customer there. John du Monceau was the CEO of Europcar, and he was justifiably angry about the service he was getting. Similarly, our account team there was angry because they saw themselves as fulfilling their obligations and getting no credit for that. It was a standoff and they were frozen in place.

I listened to our team describe their frustration at being able to deal with John and his Europcar team when I first got to Paris. We had a meeting scheduled with John and his leaders at their headquarters in Saint-Quentin which was outside of Paris near Versailles. There were a lot of issues in the dispute, but the big one was that the Perot Systems team saw the IT systems performing poorly because they did not have enough storage. To add an appropriate level of storage to make the systems perform well would cost four million dollars. Both sides agreed on that. In the contract, hardware was the financial responsibility of the customer, but Europcar was refusing to agree to spend the money to expand the hardware computer system with the storage. Their position was that the software was inefficient and that Perot Systems should fix that. So the discussions were at an impasse, and Europcar was experiencing poor systems performance which was negatively impacting their business. Our team described John as an emotional Frenchman who would not stand up to his obligations in the contract and who was demanding that Perot Systems buy the expanded storage with their funds.

My experience in business disputes is that most of the time, there is responsibility on both sides. I knew of John du Monceau's background, and he was a serious senior international business leader; clearly, you do not rise to that level if you are driven by emotions as our team described. I also knew that the method by which you express frustration and how you negotiate varies by country and culture. The rest of the world sees the United States as the most litigious society in the world. They see us as driven by attorneys and not by proper business relationships. I knew that in Europe, it took longer to enter into business relationships than it did in the United States, but once you were working together, those relationships lasted longer than in the United States. Overall, the business environment was just as vibrant as the United States, but the processes were decidedly different than in the United States. I went into the first meeting with Europcar with this in mind and also went in with the lessons from my grandfather in mind—build a personal relationship before you do business.

The first meeting with Europcar was memorable. Our team, accompanied by our general counsel, was there on one side of the conference table. On the other side were the Europcar leaders. John du Monceau, as appropriate, was at the head of the table. The only smile on any face in the room was on mine as I introduced myself to the Europcar people. John was gracious in getting everyone seated and in place. Then, he started his opening speech. It was incredible! He went through the entire relationship with Perot Systems and outlined what they had done for Europcar and what Europcar had done for them. I could see he was building a case that the relationship was in trouble. Now, his style was expressive and forceful. He demonstrated the pain that he had endured due to the impasse, but he also demonstrated his commitment to the relationship. He was loud, at times—very loud—and acted out his frustration as he walked around the room.

I almost laughed at one point when he was contrasting the French and United States way of doing business. He pointed out that years ago, when the Perot Systems executives first came to visit Europcar, he hosted them and took them to lunch at a private room at a fine French restaurant. He reeled off the menu—foie gras, salmon, wines, etc. He, then, talked about his visit to the Dallas headquarters of Perot Systems where he said they brought lunch into the conference room and fed him "hamburgers and a Coca-Cola!" Yes, business methods do vary.

He said the United States was too litigious and that that business people should make business decisions, not attorneys. He said that we should act in the "spirit of the deal" rather than blindly following the contact. He closed by asking us to purchase the four million dollars in new storage hardware since that was the quickest way to improve the overall system performance.

I glanced over at our team from Perot Systems. They were listening, but they had heard this before, and they were angry. I could see the veins bulging on the necks of most of them. Several were gripping the edge of the table. Clearly, they were frustrated and near exploding.

As John du Monceau was talking, I was listening, but I was also thinking about how I could build a respectful and trusting relationship with this business leader. That was the key. Once we had such a relationship, we could solve problems together. I was remembering the lessons of my grandfather.

After John finished his forty-five-minute speech, he sat down at the head of the table and crossed his arms. That was obviously not a sign of openness or flexibility.

I took a deep breath before I said anything and reminded myself that I should not say the words contract or lawyer in my remarks. I needed to talk business, not legalese, to resolve this situation. I pointedly sat in my chair and did not rise to speak to lessen the tension.

I began by thanking John for bringing me up-to-date on the situation, and I told him that I appreciated the background information he gave me. I did not use the "I feel your pain" line from Bill Clinton, but that was the tone of my remarks. I acknowledged that their business had suffered and said that was not acceptable. I pointed out that Perot Systems business had also suffered. I reiterated several of the points he had raised as examples of opportunities to work together to improve our businesses that had been lost over time. I said that I was here, and my primary job was to change the business relationship between Europcar and Perot Systems so that it was working for both parties. I said we would put all issues on the table and would work with him to resolve them quickly so that both of our businesses could get healthier. I closed by saying it would be nice if we could delegate this task to our teams to work out the details, but I did not think that would work. So I proposed that John and I sit down together to work on this and that we have these regular meetings face-to-face. I told him that I was committed to doing this and wanted to start the next day by returning to meet privately with him. He nodded and said that was good.

He, then, asked, "Is there any way that you could buy the disk drives (the additional storage)?"

I said, "Yes, that is possible. If the two of us agree on how we get this business relationship back on track so that our businesses will no longer suffer as they are today, I can see us purchasing that storage as part of a broader business agreement."

John said, "That is the right thing for you to do. This is a good start. Let us work together as businessmen. That is the European way versus the US way." He stood up, walked over to my seat, and extended his hand. I stood and shook his hand.

In the parking lot after the meeting, as our team walked to their cars, they expressed two views; first, they were amazed that I was able to speak respectfully to John and that he spoke respectfully to me, and second, they were angry at me for "agreeing to buy the storage."

I said, "Listen, guys. This contract is worth tens of millions of dollars to us a year, and it is a long-term contract. But it is on the edge of blowing up. If you look at all that we have on the line, four million dollars is not a deal-breaker, one way or the other. Yes, Europcar wants us to pay the four million dollars, and that is not in the contract, but we want them to do things with us that are worth far more to us than that amount. Let's solve these issues broadly and systemically. We need to be driven by creating business value for our company as well as for Europcar, not mechanically following a contract and letting it limit our creativity and progress. Yes, we have to follow the contact and business model, but when it no longer fits the business, let's renegotiate it so that it does."

I started meeting with John, and we made remarkable progress. The contractual business structure had outlived its usefulness. He wanted a list of things changed as did we. We put them all on the table and negotiated an amendment to the contract. It gave both of us business flexibility that we wanted, and it fit our then-current needs. It allowed John to build Europcar into a bigger success. It allowed Perot Systems to have a relationship with far more profit in it than previously. It was the single largest contributor to our annual profits that year and for several years afterward. And yes, as part of that agreement, we did purchase the four million dollars in storage. It was a win-win negotiation, but it could never have happened if John and I had not first built a personal relationship. I respect John and have always spoken highly of him as a business leader.

After we concluded our negotiations, John took me to a magnificent lunch at a high-end French restaurant; and hamburgers were not on the menu.

Now, I will warn you that you can take the caring too far and get too deep in someone's personal life. When I was at EDS, they had a contract to develop and install a new customer service and billing system for Northeast Utilities, a very large regional electricity provider in the 1970s that was headquartered in Hartford, Connecticut. EDS also was developing and installing a big construction management system at the same time for Northeast Utilities. These contracts were among the first in the utility industry, so everyone wanted to make them go perfectly as they would, then, be the basis for attracting other customers.

This division was headed by a vice president, Glen Self, of whom you have already heard a lot about. Due to the importance of these new projects and due to Glen's insistence on always getting the best people for every endeavor, he hand selected a special team to go to the SED Phase II training as a class and, then, to move to Hartford to build that customer service and billing system. I was selected as a part of this special class.

Once we got to Connecticut and began work, we had to get organized. EDS had taken us rookies and added a number of more senior people to our team. Everyone was eager to see who would get what roles on the team. I was selected to be a team leader, and my team was made up primarily of these more experienced people as well as a couple from our class. At first, I was amazed that I was selected to be the team leader of people decades older and more experienced than me. I was in my twenties, and they were in their forties or fifties. I was flattered and resolved to do the best job that I could. Parenthetically, I learned later that most of the senior technical people did not want to be the team leader because the team leader had to talk with customers. Working with machines was more comfortable for these technically talented people rather than working with people. But youngster that I was, I took the job because I was comfortable working with people.

The not-to-follow leadership lesson that I will tell you occurred when I was promoted to be leader of this entire project. One of the senior technical people, a very solid performer, came to me to say that he thought he was underpaid. I told him that I would get some data on that and would respond to his request for a raise. When I did the research, it showed that he was fairly paid as he was. I took that information back to him, and we had a robust discussion on it. We, then, talked about what he could do to be even more valuable and earn additional compensation. At the end of the discussion, he said he was convinced that he was fairly paid, but he had a special request for me. He said, "I see that I am paid fairly, but my wife has been on me to make more since our kids are in college, and we need the extra income. Would you talk with her like you did with me so that you can help me convince her?" I should have declined this request, but as an inexperienced business leader, I told him that I would do this. Dumb.

We made an appointment, and in a few days, he brought his wife in to see me. I was stunned. This lady was like my mother! She was about the same age, and she had kids in college where I was just a few years ago. I was taken aback by her and had to recover during the conversation. Somehow, I got through it, and with a combination of data, genuineness, and sheer luck, I made it through the conversation with her successfully.

My primary learning from these events, however, was that you can take personal engagement with your team too far—way too far—and if you do so, that will not work. There needs to be some distance between leaders and people, and you need to maintain that respectful distance.

Get to know your team as individuals but maintain a bit of distance when you are a leader. Don't do what I did and get involved in marriage counseling.

Information Technology Icon: Bill Gayden

Bill Gayden was smart. To be specific, you would call him street-smart. He was quick-witted; he knew how to read people; he knew how to negotiate; and he knew how to sell.

Bill was one of the original VPs at EDS, and for most of his career, he led their sales functions. He was also the leader who started a lot of their new things. One thing he started for EDS was their international business, and he ran that division for a number of years. He was in charge of international and specifically the business in Iran when EDS pulled off the feat of rescuing two of their team who were in jail after the government of the Shah of Iran fell in the 1970s. You can read more about this inspiring business story in Ken Follett's book, *On Wings of Eagles*. Bill was in Tehran when the operation was in place and has some great stories about it.

One thing I learned from Bill is the ability to work on several levels of intangibility at the same time. He would be in conversation with you about inconsequential things like talking about sports, but all the while, he was sizing you up and planning his business approach. I saw this most vividly when I was at EDS and was part of a project to propose software development services to the government of Pakistan. The team spent several weeks in Pakistan, working with government officials and key partners such as IBM. Bill flew into Karachi to meet us and to negotiate with the IBM country manager. He checked into the hotel and suggested that we have the meeting in the bar rather than in a conference room, saying that he wanted to get to know the IBM leader. We had drinks (several rounds) in the bar and did a lot of talking about everything but the project in Pakistan for several hours. When everyone was tiring and about ready to leave, Bill suddenly switched topics and said, "Here is how I see us working together on this." He pulled out a napkin and sketched the business relationship, pricing, exchange of value parameters, and key messages. It was incredible and spot on! All of the time in the bar, while most of us were focused on the small talk, Bill was leading the small talk but was also thinking and planning on another level—the business deal.

This is a key ability you need to have, particularly if you are in sales or are a corporate leader who is working to make deals happen. Keep that in mind as you have future meetings or sales calls—everyone can work on one level; you need to work on multiple levels at the same time.

After EDS, Bill Gayden ran Ross Perot's oil business, Petrus, and then later, founded and ran Merit Energy which is one of the best run investment partnerships in the oil business. Not many people are hugely successful in multiple industries, but he was.

Ron as an EDS employee in Pakistan at the confluence
of the Indus and Kabul Rivers in 1977

Answer every question

Our son, David Nash, was selecting a topic to write about for
a college application. One essay question on the application was
"Describe a situation when you learned a lot and talk about how
you learn." Most people would take this as an opportunity to promote themselves by choosing a time when they had a learned teacher
who taught them about a difficult subject. David took the opposite
approach and talked about how he learned as a young child. In doing
so, he wrote a touching and revealing essay about himself. And, he
impressed the admissions committee in doing so as they accepted his
application.

One evening, David and I were driving home from an event. It
was just after dinner, and David was about six or seven years old. It
was getting dark as we were driving, and he noticed a bright streak
of light in the sky, and like most children, he asked, "What is that
bright light?" It was from a spotlight that was raking the sky. Once I
told him that, he asked, "How does it work?" We, then, went into a
discussion of arc lights (versus lightbulbs) and how they work. That
led to talking about how electricity works. Finally, as we were driving
and talking, I asked if he would like to see if we could drive around
to find the source of the spotlight. He enthusiastically said, "Yes!"

We were driving around north Dallas and made a lot of twists and turns as we tried to get to the spot where the spotlight originated. He loved the chase. We finally came down the street and saw the spotlight—at a newly opened McDonald's! This was great. We got to walk up to see the spotlight in action and, then, to go to McDonald's to have some French fries and a drink. What a fun evening.

I forgot about this night, but David did not. As he aged, he remembered it as a time when he asked a lot of questions about something that he did not understand, and it resulted in his gaining an understanding of spotlights and electricity. That is a powerful lesson of learning. Don't be afraid to ask questions, and you will be surprised at how much you can learn. This essay got David into a great college, and his self-awareness is a trait that he maintains today.

Two important and necessary traits of a leader are self-awareness and an ability to learn. Both of these traits are required for a great success. Don't ever get so self-important that you stop asking questions and stop learning. If you do, that will mean your career will only go backward from there.

Treat people with respect in their world

Raising children is a tough job, but it is one of the most rewarding things you can do in life. I heartily recommend that everyone get married and raise children if they can. You will benefit greatly as a person and as a leader by doing so.

Sometimes, your children do things that are so caring and spectacular that they just take your breath away. Our daughter, Stacey Nash Thompson, did that once, and I learned an important leadership lesson from her. We were at a wedding reception for a couple which our family knew, and there was a significant difference in the economic standing of the families of the bride and the groom. One of the couple was raised pretty wealthy and one was from a good family living in a community that struggled economically.

At this reception, my back was turned, and I heard a young girl say to my daughter, "Stacey, that is a beautiful dress, did you get it at Target or Walmart?" Now, I knew that my fashion-leading daughter from Dallas had spent far more than prices at those stores on her dress, but I was worried about how she would respond. My ears perked up, and I heard her say, "No, I did not get it from either of them, I got my dress from a local store in Dallas." The young girl said that was fine; she just really liked the dress and thought she might find one like it someday.

Now, the reason I was so proud of my daughter was that I knew she got the dress at Neiman Marcus in Dallas. That is an expensive store, but it is a "local store" as she said. What a great way to give the other person the respect she deserved in answering the question. I was so happy that Stacey was perceptive enough to give such a respectful answer.

The leadership lesson in this is that as a leader, you owe each member of your team respect, regardless of their economic circumstances, their position, or their performance. When I work late at night and am leaving while the janitorial crew is cleaning the offices, I try to always speak to them respectfully. They are doing a tough job, and they deserve just as much respect as any of our team. Without them, we all would fail pretty quickly.

A colleague and good friend of mine, Berry Cash, had a true story which he told when he was interviewing candidates coming from big jobs at a big company to take a job as a CEO of a start-up company. Berry was at a board meeting of a small company one day, when they heard someone yelling in the hallway. After a couple of yells, they stopped the board meeting to walk down the hall. They heard someone from one of the unisex bathrooms yelling that there was no toilet paper in the restroom and asking someone to give them a roll. The CEO walked down the hall to the other bathroom, but it also had no toilet paper. He, then, walked to the break room to get some. None was there either. He, then, walked with great formality to a list on the wall and told the board, "Each week, one of our team is assigned the duty to go to Walmart to pick up toilet paper, Cokes, snack bars, etc. Let's see who messed up and did not do their work this week." The name on the list for that week was the CEO's. He had neglected to get the supplies for everyone.

Berry's point was that if you are so wrapped up in your own importance that you cannot envision yourself going to Walmart and filling the trunk of your car with supplies, then, you don't need to be working in a start-up; just stay in the big company that has staff for such duties.

The larger leadership lesson is to never forget that you are just one member of the team. You have an important job but so does each and every member of your team. You owe them respect in every interaction with them. If they fail, you fail. Don't ever forget that.

Show a genuine interest in other people

My wife, Susan Nash, is an excellent leader. She has many leadership skills that I have observed over the years. One of the most powerful ones that I see is that she connects with people incredibly quickly. She forms strong bonds of trust quicker than most leaders I see. That is a great leadership quality, and I have observed her for a long time to see how she does this.

She forms that bond by taking a genuine interest in each person she meets. She may only be sitting next to someone on an airplane, but when she turns to talk to them, she wants to get to know them. She wants to know something about them, rather than wants to impress the person with her achievements. That is a great way to bond with people—show a genuine interest in them first. You cannot fake this; it has to be genuine.

Susan starts every conversation with a stranger by asking about them; where are you from, where are you going on this trip? I have seen her get people to open up and reveal themselves quickly even when you have just sat down with them at dinner. At first, I thought it was one of her trick questions like, "Where did you two meet before you married?" That always opens up people and gets them to talk about the essence of themselves. But I have come to realize that is it not the trick question; it is the fact that Susan absolutely wants to understand something about the person she just met. It is a powerful bonding agent.

If you can be interested first in other people, you will learn what they are like, what they want to do, what they can do, what they are afraid of, etc. You will, then, be so much better equipped to have these people join your team, and you will understand how to get them to do their best. Think about changing your first interaction from one where you promote yourself to one where you learn about others. You will be smarter and more successful by doing so.

Let your people get to know you

Every first-time leader, except the true idiots, understands that they are in a new position for which they are not completely prepared. They want the position, and they want to succeed, but they are still scared. One of their big worries is that the team they are leading will realize they are scared, so some new leaders try to put on a façade of experience when they really do not have it. This is very dangerous.

As a leader, you need to be calm and to project strength. But never forget that you are a person just like your team. Don't make yourself inhuman; it is not you, and your team will see through it.

In the military, there is a separation between the enlisted people, the noncommissioned officers, and the commissioned officers. There is a reason for separations, and the military prescribes various non-solicitation rules for each group. There are good reasons for this and some great leadership lessons that you can learn from this.

A simple but important lesson to learn as a leader comes from a military tradition. Once you have a dinner, then, you go to the bar for drinks. The commanding officer goes to the bar with his team and buys the first round. When that round is over, the commanding officer clears the tab and heads back to his quarters. You don't want to be around for what happens when the team consumes excess alcohol. I've told this to many business leaders. You want to be friends but have limits. Be one of the team but know when to separate yourself. This tradition from the military is one that you should use in your business career.

There are some necessary separations between leaders and their people. But it is also empowering for your team to see you as a human being, not as a robot. They want to have confidence in you as a leader, but they also want to have confidence in you as a thinking and feeling human being.

I was in the Old Guard in the military, the infantry unit of the army that performs ceremonial duties in Arlington National Cemetery and at the White House. They have a very strict way to dress, to march, and even to walk. They are the most strict unit in the army in these matters. Years after I was in the Old Guard, I took my wife and son to see a parade at Fort Myer in Washington, D.C. They were impressed by the ceremony and had a number of other reactions. My son said, "Dad, I always thought you were relaxed and approachable, but sometimes, you just stiffened up and were very unapproachable. Seeing how the Old Guard marches, I now understand. In certain circumstances, you revert to that formal stiffness. I never understood that part of you until today."

So this is an example of opening up and revealing yourself. My son never understood a part of my nature until he saw from where I came. Isn't that incredible?

Your team needs to get to know you. Don't bore them with vacation photos or such, but let them know that you have a family, that you have outside interests, etc. Let them know of your background, and they will understand you better and be more comfortable with you. Keep your separation as needed but do not hide your humanity. If they do not see you as a feeling human being, they will think you are a harsh automaton. That is not a good positioning for a leader.

Be aware of cultural differences in international business

I had the opportunity to do business with people around the world throughout my career, and that has been a great benefit to my development as a leader since the business culture differs by country. Like most Americans, I grew up unilingual and did not learn a second or third language. The advantage of being a native English speaker is that business people around the world generally know English and can speak with you in that language. The disadvantage of being only an English speaker is that people are talking to you in their second or third language, which means you are not getting the most robust perception of them as you interact. Therefore, you have to go the extra mile and take active steps to get to know people in international settings.

Once, I went to the United Kingdom and had a local member of my team who had set up multiple interviews with business people for us to get some feedback on a new product idea we had. We were in the very early stages of the sales cycle and wanted to test our messaging and value propositions with some business people who might later move into the sales cycle as prospects. The first three visits went as expected; my team member would open the meeting, tell the business executive why we were there, introduce me as the CEO of the company, and tee up the discussion for me. We got a lot of good feedback from those sessions.

We went into the fourth meeting that day, and things went differently. When we were escorted to the office of the business executive, we sat down, and then, my team member was mute; no introduction, no teeing me up, etc. He just sat there. After a period of awkward silence, I jumped in to give his pitch and, then, continued with my portion. My team member was quiet except to answer a couple of pointed questions from the business executive. After we left the building, I asked him, "What went on in there? Why were you mute? Why didn't you do the introduction?"

He said, "It was not appropriate for me to step out and lead the meeting with the business executive."

"Why?" I asked.

"He went to Cambridge, and I did not attend Cambridge or Oxford for university."

"What difference does that make?"

"If I had aggressively tried to sell him, he would have just blown us off. It would not be good manners for me to deal with him that way. The appropriate way for me to deal with him was to just answer questions, not to try to sell him or push him."

"Wow," I said. As I thought about what he said, I thought it was ridiculous (from an American perspective), but this guy was a senior sales leader, so he knew his craft. Then, I switched to wondering why he did not warn me that this visit was going to be different and that I would have to carry the whole load by myself. I asked, "Why didn't you tell me you were going to be mute before we got there"

His surprising reply was, "I did not know he was a Cambridge guy until we got into his office."

"I did not see a diploma on the wall, did you see him wearing a ring or something?"

"No, it was the way he spoke."

I was stunned. That was a level of social and business hierarchy that I had never dealt with in the United States. Sure, some executives are arrogant, but I did not know any that expected people to alter their behavior this much. This was one of my early lessons in the differences that local business cultures could make. It was an important lesson for me to be more perceptive when talking with international business executives.

I learned this again when I was at Perot Systems and had interviewed a candidate for a sales leadership role in our company. I was running Europe, and this candidate was German. I was interviewing him in our office in Niederrad, near Frankfurt, Germany. During the interview (conducted in English), I thought he was experienced and smart but very tentative and certainly not aggressive enough for a sales leader. But my German team thought otherwise. They encouraged me to spend more time with him and to go to dinner with him and several of them. We did, and the language at the table was English for most of the dinner, but a few times, it switched to German. When it did, I noticed a sea change in the candidate's personality; he was confident, outgoing, funny, etc. I did not see any of that in the interview. When the language switched back to English, his demeanor became passive again.

I was discussing this the next day with our German team. They laughed. One of them even said, "We know this. All of the American leaders hire the Germans with the best English-speaking skills, no matter what their qualifications are."

That was a big lesson. I made two changes after that:

1. I resolved to always have a group interview as part of the process and to observe that group interview in the native language of the candidate. Then, I could see their real demeanor.
2. I resolved to always have a native team member with me in business meetings in foreign countries. When you are selling or negotiating, there is a thin margin for error. You cannot miss many signals, or you will not get the result you want. Assume that you are going to miss 15 percent of the signals if you are not a native; that is more than the margin of error. So have someone with you who is picking up those signals so that you can succeed in business transactions.

I saw this need again once as our German Perot Systems team was preparing for a meeting with me and a high-ranking German business executive of Hamburg Mannheimer. Our internal team met the prior afternoon and evening to get our slide presentation ready. Our German team had hundreds of potential sides, diving into minute detail. I insisted that I would only take in six slides, printed on paper, so that we could have a strategic executive discussion. I would not subject the executive to even fifty slides presented on a screen as he sat in the dark. I knew I was right on the format, so I held my ground. We were still working on slides at 2:00 a.m. when I finally told them I was going to bed. I had my six slides, and they could work all night on the details if they wanted, but I wanted to be fresh for our 8:00 a.m. meeting.

Our senior German sales leader and I went to meet the business executive. His English speaking was superb, and we were having a very positive discussion. The six pages of information were just right, and they sparked the right level of engagement. The sales call was going very well. The business executive asked a very detailed question, and I was about to answer him with more specificity than was on the slides, when our German sales leader quietly placed his hand on my arm to quiet me. He leaned over to his huge briefcase where he had the two hundred slides printed out. He thumbed through that pile, withdrew the slide with the information on it, and handed it to the business executive. We presented the answer on that slide and answered his question. The sales call was positive and moved the process along.

After leaving the building, I asked the German sales leader, "Why did you take the time to dive through all of those slides when I knew the answer and could have quickly told him?"

His reply was, "It was a test. He wanted to know if we had really thought out our business proposition to him. Showing him that we had prepared hundreds of slides and had really worked the details was the message he wanted to hear, not the answer to the specific question."

That was perceptive and showed me that I had missed a critical part of the sale process. But the local German sales leader saw the game that was going on and handled it properly.

The lesson for a leader is to not assume that everyone around the world does business just like we do in the United States. You need to take the time to learn the local business customs and taking a local with you is a great way to make sure you don't miss something.

One final lesson on international business processes that I learned involves expectations and metrics. At Teleci, I was leading the company, and we had imported a new product from Hitachi in Japan. Hitachi had only sold this product in Japan, so they had to do the internationalization for it and needed a business case to support it. They asked us at Teleci for a forecast of how many units we though we could sell the first year and subsequent years.

We worked as best we could to get a tight estimate and sent that over to Japan. That was enough volume for them to justify the project, and we got started. They did the modifications, and soon, we had a product. We worked really hard that first year to get this product adopted and reach our goals. It was very difficult, at first, because we had no references of anyone in the United States who had ever used this product, so we got behind our forecast. But we closed strongly and got to 96 percent of our forecast for the year. We celebrated because we really had no idea how many we could sell, and we got very close to our estimate for the first year, and the momentum that we had made us confident that we would exceed the estimate for the second year.

The lead executive from Hitachi in Japan for this division was coming over for his first visit to our office shortly after the end of that first year. We laid on a lot of things for him to do and scheduled a great celebratory party at the end to commemorate our successful first year.

When the Japanese executive arrived, he was very gracious and cordial. When I had the first one-on-one time with him in my office, however, his demeanor changed. He was furious that we had *missed* our forecast by 4 percent and wanted to know what financial compensation we were planning to give them.

I was stunned. The forecast had been a shot in the dark, and we almost made it. We had sold millions of dollars of product for him and had a great pipeline for far more in the second year. We thought it was a big success as a new product introduction. He thought it was a failure.

I asked him, and he talked about how he had told his bosses in Japan the forecast and that missing any forecast, even by a little amount, is a huge career-threatening deed in Japan. We discussed it, and his view was just very opposed to ours. We had done as good an estimate as we could with no hard information and sent him that forecast. He wanted a number that was rock solid, even if it was a far lower number. We were looking at longer-term business success, and he was looking only at that first year and making that estimate.

Obviously, we should have discounted by a large safety factor before giving him the estimate. That intense focus on the short term, in our opinion, would limit your flexibility to respond to changing business conditions, but we did not understand his world when we were giving him information.

The leadership lesson is to make sure you understand the business world of your partner or your customer. Don't assume that they will react just like a partner or customer in the United States. If you don't know the target, it is tough to hit the bullseye. Understand international business cultures so that you can target and achieve success. That is how you become a success as an international business leader.

EPILOGUE AND CHALLENGE

If you have read this far, you now know a lot about how you lead in various business situations. You also know a lot about the information technology industry and some key leaders in it. That is nice. But the question is what are you going to do with this new knowledge?

You have to be committed to developing yourself as a leader, and you have to work this process as a priority for decades. You can never stop learning to be a better leader. Just reading a book will not make you a leader; you have to show this commitment by intense focus on improving over a long period of time. If you don't, you can lead people, but you will not be the success that you want to be.

You have to be committed and take the actions to improve yourself on multiple skills. Without an objective view of yourself and a commitment to learn, practice, and improve, you will not make it. You cannot grow without being great at self-improvement.

You have to learn and practice the skills of leadership until they become habits. Business is intellectually tough to master, and you cannot master it if you are simultaneously thinking about what leadership skill you should be using. These skills need to become second nature or muscle memory to use a sports analogy. Focus on learning and practicing them one at a time, as that is the best way to embed them in your persona.

You have to drive yourself maniacally in order to be a good leader. You cannot deal with issues and people by brief flyovers at thirty thousand feet in the air. You have to grab hold of the details and stand shoulder to shoulder with your team members. You have to outwork them and show them the best role model for full commitment to making the business a success. Leading is not an easier job than working; it is a tougher job when done well.

Finally, you have to realize that it is not all about you, and you have to focus on making your team and your team members a big success. Leaders succeed when their teams win. The best leaders have the best people because people flock to leaders who will develop and promote them. Helping others succeed helps you succeed. No successful leader is an egotist who is out for themselves. Team members see through that and avoid such leaders. Be a servant leader; your team will succeed and so will you.

You now understand my path to becoming a leader. I still, however, learn things every day. I have been lucky enough to have attracted very talented teams to work with me all throughout my career. They have pushed me upward; I did not claw my way to the top. My teams deserve the credit for everything that I have accomplished.

I hope you decide to work to become a leader. It is a very fun and very rewarding job when you do it right. If you are committed and you follow the practices correctly, you can do it. Just understand that it is a long-term commitment for long-term success. At this point of her TV show, Julia Child would look at the audience and end by saying, "Bon appetit!" I will end by saying, "Good leading!"

ABOUT THE AUTHOR

Ron Nash was a talented kid who grew up in the suburbs of Atlanta as the son of an electrical engineer. He was oriented toward technology from an early age. He left high school early after winning academic scholarships to both universities to which he applied—Georgia Tech and MIT. As a sixteen-year-old, he chose to stay closer to home and attend Georgia Tech.

In addition to his academic prowess, he also developed and excelled as a leader in organizations starting from a young age. The combination of detailed technology knowledge/skills and the people-oriented skills of leadership propelled him in his career.

After college and a stint in the US Army in their elite infantry unit, The Old Guard, in Washington, D.C., he joined Ross Perot during the go-go days of EDS, a pioneering company that invented the information technology services industry. His success there allowed him to leave and earn executive leadership positions as president of multiple technology companies.